CW00430817

THE KINDER LOG

Cover illustration: The Woolpacks, Kinder Scout.
Photo: Mike Williams Photography.

The fascinating Whipsnade area of Kinder Scout.

THE KINDER LOG

T.NELTHORPE

Photographs by John Woodhouse.

CICERONE PRESS,
MILNTHORPE, CUMBRIA

© T.Nelthorpe 1987
ISBN 0902363-91-3

CONTENTS

Acknowledgement

My thanks are due to Mr. Ron Collier for permission to use information from his book *The Dark Peak Aircraft Wrecks* (Wharncliffe Woodmoor, 1982).

INTRODUCTION

The Kinder Log is a handbook to the topography and history of one of Britain's favourite mountains. Kinder Scout (2088ft.) is a region of dark peat moorland in the Peak District bounded to the north by the A57 (Snake Pass) road and to the south by the Edale Valley and Chinley. Derwent Vale limits it to the east and Hayfield to the west. If we count the following as key access points - Nether Booth, Edale End, Jaggers Clough, Crookstone Hill, Rowlee Bridge, Blackden Barn, Snake Inn, Snake Summit, Hurst Reservoir, Bray Clough, Grouse Inn, Carr Meadow, Hayfield, Peep o' Day, South Head, Brown Knoll, Horsehill Tor, Lee Farm, Barber Booth and Edale, then the total area is 35-45sq. miles (45-60sq. kms.). The total area of Kinder Scout itself is 22-26sq. miles (29-35sq. kms.) and the summit plateau, triangular in shape, is approximately 14sq. miles (21sq. kms.). To walk round the massif is about 25 miles (40 kms.). (See Walk 17)

The moor is a product of the classic Pennine domal structure. The deep underlying rock is limestone upon which is laid gritstone. The gritstone erodes into wierd tors and edges and is itself overlaid with a thick blanket of peat. Savage erosion dissects this with channels known as *groughs,* usually 5 to 15ft. deep, which can make walking arduous. The Plateau has been compared with the Somme battlefield in the way it is eroded. At the southern end the vale of Edale is made of shales; softer beds interposed between the gritstone and the limestone which appears at Castleton.

A number of walks, mostly of medium length, are included in this book. They are intended to give a visitor a good picture of the mountain, but it should be noted that the weather on Kinder can be less than kind. In winter it can be very severe indeed and the high moors are then suitable only for properly equipped and experienced parties. An ability to use map and compass is useful at all times. Emergency food should always be carried and in winter a torch is essential.

Just because Kinder Scout is not dramatic like Tryfan or Gable, don't assume it is an easy mountain. Too many walkers have made that mistake in the past and paid for it with their lives.

Looking south east across the Fair Brook to Seal Edge on Kinder Scout.

THE KINDER LOG

The Kinder Log deals with the land on and around Kinder Scout, in fact it is really an A - Z of Kinder with a bit of folklore and legend added here and there. I have also included places near and far which have a relevant bearing on the history of the Scout, and for good measure I have also included a few characters and animals associated with the Scout.

All the places mentioned can be located with the relevant grid number which is found alongside each main heading, all the grid numbers can be located on the Ordnance Survey map *The Dark Peak 1/25,000.* Whilst you are out walking, you may find it hard to locate one or two places, but persevere for they *are* there.

Where the year follows the name of a certain place, it shows when the place in question became known in its pronunciation and spelling as it stands today.

Be warned - do not try to locate off the beaten track places in bad weather, for there is always another day.

—A—

AE - DAEL (see Edale)
AIDELE (see Edale)
ALDER BROOK (see Oller Brook)
ANSON (see Aircraft Crash Sites, two references)
AQUA DE ESHOP (see River Ashop)
AQUA DE ESSOP (see River Ashop)

ASHOP CLOUGH (1840) GR.090907
Centuries ago this clough went by a different name, Ash Tree Valley, so called for it was literally lined with ash trees. Alas, there are no trees to be found along this valley now until you reach the Ladyclough Plantation near the Snake Inn. The clough is three miles (5kms.) long, stretching from near the Mill Hill to near the Snake Inn. It entertains the River Ashop and the Snake Path. Certain stretches of this path are quite boggy at the best of times. However, for this minor inconvenience you are compensated by the manificent views of the Kinder escarpment. If you are travelling from Mill Hill along this sodden path then, upon reaching the old ruined shooting cabin near to the Upper Gate Clough your fortunes change for the better. The ground underfoot improves considerably and the land around you also changes dramatically. You have entered a world of beauty, with the deep chasm that the River Ashop meanders through, to the cascading mini waterfalls beneath the coniferous trees of the Saukin Ridge, then onto the end of the valley which widens out before you, a welcome sight after walking over mud and clay earlier on.

ASHOP HEAD (1627) GR.066906
The summit of this area is 1761 feet (536m) high. The head lies just below the Western buttress of the Scout, and the terrain consists of a thick messy sodden bog of peat; though I can think of a stronger word for it. The name is derived from the source of the River Ashop where it starts its meandering journey through the Ashop Clough. Across this bog the Snake Path travels, so be very wary where you tread, or you may find your legs encased up to your thighs in sodden peat. Be especially wary in very misty weather for this region is not flat but rather humpy, with deep cut peat channels.

ASHOP MOOR (1850) GR.135885
A rugged moor lacking in beauty, it lies just below Blackden Edge overlooking the splendid Woodlands Valley. The main access point

for this region is located down by Blackden Barn. A number of minor tributaries run down off this moor to help swell the River Ashop below.

ASH TREE VALLEY (see Ashop Clough)
ASTON (see Kinder Parishes)

—B—

BACKSIDE WOOD GR.156873
Thinly wooded area which leads to the access point of open country via Jaggers Clough, and not as the name seemingly implies to a certain part of one's anatomy!

BAGSHAW BRIDGE GR.162863
The last bridge on the eastern side of Edale in the Parish of Hope, or vice versa the first bridge in the Parish of Hope at Edale End. The bridge was named after a certain Phillip Bagshaw in the year 1658 and was erected to ford the River Noe to gain access to Edale End. Nowadays it is also used to gain access to open country beyond Edale End, be it either Kinder, Win Hill or over to the Ladybower dams and reservoirs.

BAGSHAW, PHILLIP (see Bagshaw Bridge)
BAKESTONE DELPH CLOUGH (see Bray Clough)

BARBER BOOTH (1675) GR.114847
Formerly Whitemoorley Booth, Whitemoreley (1579) and Whitmorlie Booth (1625). Renamed Barber Booth in 1675 after a well known family of the locality with the surname Barber - though it has been open to discussion as to whether this is the original site of Barber Booth. It is a small quaint hamlet at the western end of the Vale of Edale, accessible via the main thoroughfare through the Vale, which then carries on up to Mam Tor, Mam Nick and Rushup Edge. Campers might note that there is a small but convenient grocer's shop located in the Booth.

BASHFORD MR. & MRS. (see Mountain View)
BESINGWEAL ABBEY (see Edale Cross)

BIG AND LITTLE BUTTRESS GR.093898
One of the largest of the rocky outcrops found along the Edge, a

veritable playground for rock climbers, both experienced and novices. Exceptional views from here over the Ashop Valley.

BLACK ASHOP EDGE (see Kinder Edge)

BLACK ASHOP MOOR GR.090903
Frightening in mist, but pleasant on bright sunny days, the moor tends to lie in the shadows most of the day, hence the name. The moor is made up of steep sided flanks reaching up to the Kinder Edge. Cutting their way through these steep sides are a number of tributaries which either flow from or near to the summit, down the moor where they marry up with the River Ashop in the valley below.

BLACKDEN BARN GR.130894
Formerley Blackden End. A private barn in an area of no access, it does serve as a good landmark for either gaining or exiting at the boundary of open country. This point lies above a footbridge which fords the River Ashop below Dean Hill. The barn is easily located from any decent vantage point, but a word of warning is necessary - the barn is situated in a remote place. It is a long way to the nearest town, village, hamlet or public transport, unless however you plan to hitch a lift along the Snake road.

BLACKDEN EDGE GR.132894
This edge overlooks the scenic Woodlands Valley, and from the same viewpoint you can also gaze out and take in the natural landslip and formation of the splendid Alport Castles. The length of Blackden Edge is approximately 1½ miles (2½km.) long starting at the Blackden Rind Waterfall and ending at the Crookstone Knoll. Midway along the edge is the start/finish of the 'Seven Minute Crossing', the narrowest part to cross the summit.

BLACKDEN END (see Blackden Barn)

BLACKDEN MOOR AND BROOK (1627) GR.115885
The upper regions of this moor are quite rocky, falling away to give green pasture land below. The moor is split by a large ravine through which the Blackden Brook flows on its meandering and cascading journey into the Woodlands Valley, where it joins up in matrimony with the River Ashop. Though the brook is quite pleasant an ascent up this moor via the brook's course can be very arduous and tiring.

BLACKDEN RIND GR.116884

This is one of my favourite stopping off places where I can rest up awhile. The Rind is the actual summit of the Blackden Brook which flows off the sodden peat Plateau. Located at the edge of the Rind is a small rock formation, if you stand or sit on the uppermost of these rocks you can take in some excellent views of the surrounding area. These rocks are so shaped that there is an overhang, which is most useful as shelter in very inclement weather.

BLACKESHAW HOUSE (1640) GR.067883

If you happen to be crossing Blackshaws Hill at anytime and you perceive a fine old stone farmhouse barring your way, then you will be seeing an apparition. This house was owned by a well-known local family of that era called Blackeshaw, and it was built so that it overlooked the River Kinder and the basin below which is now occupied by the Kinder Reservoir. The house was demolished well over a hundred years ago.

BLACKLEY CLOUGH (1840) GR.155883

This used to be a no access area until the National Trust obtained land around the Blackley Hey area, now the N.T. boundary line runs along the clough. The main usage of the clough is by backpackers with transport who can park below and make their way upwards to gain access to the Scout. Other users are campers who use the well-known Hagg Farm, down in the Woodlands Valley as a base. I have used this clough in very bad weather as a sort of escape route, for it runs directly down between the bases of Blackley Hey and Crookstone Hill, coming out near the Hagwater Bridge. This is the access point for the Snake Road and Hagg Farm Youth Hostel. The brook itself flows into the River Ashop close to the mouth of the Ladybower Reservoir.

BLACKLEY HEY (1627) GR.148888

A very steep hill rising sharply to the Crookstone Knoll; a picture postcard setting. The upper regions though can be very wild in windy weather. This area is confusing to some people as the access for the Hey lies half in and half out of the boundary of open access, but the problem has been eased because the N.T. has acquired a large portion of the Hey. Now the majority of the land is accessible via any footpath from the summit of Blackley Clough down to the splendid Rowlee Bridge and to within approximately 100 yards (90m.) of the River Ashop.

BLACK MOOR AND HIGH MOOR PITS GR.063923
This area lies between Hurst Moor and Glead Hill. High Moor Pits is a misleading name as there are no pits of any description here. Black Moor is an apt name for this area, for when coupled with High Moor Pits it becomes a seething mass of groughs, marsh and bog. Perhaps this is why there is no recognised path across it.

BLACK OVERHANGS GR.087898
A crag on which many a rock climber may be found hanging around. The rocks here, which are located along Kinder Edge close to the Nether Brook summit are huge slabs, black in colour, which appear to be stacked one on top of another, many overhanging.

BLACKSHAWS GR.065883
Where the River Kinder flows into the Kinder Reservoir this marks the boundary and start of Blackshaws, which is a steep banked hill facing Hollin Head. Half of Blackshaws lies in a no-access area. This area is criss-crossed with dry stone walls resulting in no recognised public right-of-way. Years ago there used to be a wooden footbridge across the River Kinder connecting Blackshaws and the once flourishing farm of Hollinhead. The upper half of this hill lies within the boundary of open access where you are free to roam.

BLACKWALL PLANTATION (1840) GR.132867
Not a plantation like it used to be years ago when this hill was half covered in magnificent conifer trees. The hill is now devoid of those, but there are a few more trees taking their place, trying once again to make this part of Edale scenic. The larger part of the Blackwall Plantation lies outside the boundary of open access, for this land is mainly grazing land for the local farms.

BOGGESWORTH (see Kinder Parishes)
BOOTH (see Farlands)

BOOTHS BRIDGE GR052882
Though this fine bridge has been renovated a few times in its two hundred years of existence, it still remains one of the main access points for entry to the moors of Kinder from Hayfield. The bridge was primarily built over the River Kinder to gain access to Booth, Upper and Lower Houses, Kinder Head and Hollin Head.

BOTHE (see Farlands)

BOWDEN BRIDGE GR.050870

A very old footbridge, probably late 16th century, which fords the River Kinder just before the meeting with the River Sett, where from this point on the name of both the rivers becomes the Sett. It is a charming spot, and a bench is conveniently situated facing this quaint bridge. I have often spent a summer evening sat on this bench after a hard day's slog of bog squelching, listening to all those sounds associated with those lovely sunny evenings.

BOWDEN BRIDGE QUARRY GR.048869

A quarry of significance, for it was here on April 24th 1932 that the infamous Kinder Trespass meeting which resulted in the Mass Trespass took place. A plaque was erected on the quarry wall in 1982 to commemorate the Trespass. The location of the quarry is easily found for it stands to one side of the Kinder Road, Hayfield, between Bowden Bridge and the Hayfield campsite. The quarry has been converted into a car park and picnic area where during the summer weekends tea and refreshments may be obtained.

BOXING GLOVE STONES GR.078897

As the name implies this unusual rock formation has the distinctive shape of a boxing glove. Be careful you do not stumble around this rock or you may find yourself out for the count of ten, as the rock stands on the Kinder Edge with a very, very long drop beneath! It is worth while stopping here to take in the magnificent views across the valley below and the moors opposite.

BRAY CLOUGH (1625), BAKESTONE DELPH CLOUGH (1840), FAIRVAGE CLOUGH GR.054918

Fairvage Clough and Bakestone Delph Clough both have small brooks which flow into the larger clough of Bray, named after a 16th century gentleman called William Braye. Fairvage is fed by a number of minor tributaries coming down off Black Moor, whilst Bray Clough is situated in a deep sided valley which is also fed by a number of tributaries both little and large. These minor water flows make up the fast flowing brook through this valley. The terrain around here leaves much to be desired, for there is a mixture of marsh, groughs, stony areas and bracken.

BRIDGE CHOCK GR.085897

A little known climbing crag found close to the Black Overhangs along the Kinder Edge. It is nothing spectacular but it is an ideal training ground for any novice climber.

BRINK (see Hope Brink)

BROAD CLOUGH (1840) GR.068872
Until the turn of the 18th century Broad Clough was known by the unusual name of Wamsbrow. The clough is not so much a clough for the basic land mass hereabouts is rather flat and lies beneath the Three Knolls. The main access point is gained via Farlands, then across farmland, for which a path is provided for your convenience. Once across the farmland you reach a dry stone wall - it is here that the boundary lines of both the open access and the N.T. are to be found.

BROADLEE BANK (see Broadlee Bank Tor)

BROADLEE BANK TOR GR.111857
When viewed from the south-west this peak resembles a mini Mam Tor. Though it is not as spectacular as Mam Tor it still holds a certain charisma of its own. The former name of the tor is a shortened version of its present name, Broadlee Bank. The tor is quite large and sticks out like an elbow into the Vale of Edale, overshadowing Barber Booth. The alternative Pennine Way route meanders along beneath its base, and whilst access to the summit can be gained from along this route it is much easier gained from walking round via the Grindsbrook Valley. The summit is pretty well flat and here you can find two quite large springs. The views are very good and they include the Great Ridge, The Vale and the South Kinder escarpment.

BRONSYDY AND BROWNESYDE (see Kinder Parishes)

BROWN KNOLL (1840) GR.084851
Standing in the Parish of Brownside this large flat topped hill is capped by an Ordnance Survey pillar, surrounded by a thick black seething mass of peat bog. Though it may be named Brown Knoll there is nothing brown of any significance here. Close by the O.S. pillar are to be found the fragments of a crashed R.A.F. Oxford plane. I would say that the only pleasing aspect of the summit is that you can take in some splendid views of the surrounding countryside, namely Kinder Low, the Vale of Edale, The Great Ridge and the land leading down to Chapel en le Frith.

BROWN KNOLL DYKE GR.084853
An undesirable ditch of boot-sucking peat and mud, which you have to cross if you wish to reach the O.S. pillar on Brown Knoll if you are coming from a northerly direction. There are one or two favourable places to cross, but during or after a rainy spell the crossing is twice as bad. The dyke follows the boundary of open access along over the Brown Knoll summit until it reaches the summit of Grain Clough.

BROWNSIDE AND BUGGESWORTHE (see Kinder Parishes)

BURNT HILL (1842) GR.045902
Not actually on Kinder but lies to the west of the Scout. Burnt Hill is on the main route from near the Grouse Inn, on the Hayfield to Glossop road. The trek over the hill takes in the Intakes, then over Burnt Hill, on over Leygatehead Moor and then onto Mill Hill, for access to the Scout. The route across this terrain is marked to a certain degree but it is not wise to attempt this crossing in any sort of mist, for it is very hard going and there are no well defined landmarks. The area is featureless. North from the summit of Burnt Hill is an O.S. pillar, standing on a hillock which goes by the name of Harry Hut.

BUXWORTH (see Kinder Parishes)

—C—

CABIN BUTTRESS GR.096898
Located on the nose of the Fairbrook Naze, this buttress represents a good challenge and playground for novice climbers. A good feature of this crag is that it offers protection in very inclement weather, for it has a very large overhang from which it gets its forename of Cabin.

CAR MEADOW (see Carr Meadow)
CARR (see Carr House)

CARR HOUSE GR.156866
Formerly Carr (1699). A small farm holding on the banks of the River Noe close to Edale Road and the railway. Accommodation is available here, but prior notice is much appreciated.

CARR MEADOW GR.035895
Formerly Car Meadow (1789). This is a long, long way from Carr house with which it has no connection. It is a pleasant little place

through which the brook from Hollingworth Clough meanders, and but for the busy A624 lying beside it, this place could quite easily become a beauty spot and picnic area for those people who like to spend a few hours in pleasant surroundings. It is situated midway along the A624 between Hayfield and Glossop or about 2 miles (3km.) south west of Mill Hill. Carr Meadow is the main access point in this region for the moors leading up to Kinder Scout. Over the brook there has been erected a fine wooden bridge in memory of one of the stalwarts of the Peak District, Thomas Boulger. There is a stone block at one end of the bridge with an inscribed tablet: *Erected in memory of THOMAS BOULGER who served the Peak District and Northern Counties Footpaths Association Society from 1921-1963.*

CATROCHE TOR (see Roych Tor)
CAVENDISH FAMILY (see Snake Inn)
CHAPEL EN LE FRITH AND CHARLESWORTH
(see Kinder Parishes)

CHENDRE GR.087876
In the Domesday Book the Normans refer to Kinder as Chendre, which translated means 'cliff of the beacon fires'. For centuries until about 1832 the moors around Kinder Scout and a very large slice of the Scout itself was known as King's Land, in other words anybody had the right to wander where they pleased without interference. This was repealed around 1832, for the land then was divided up between the landed gentry. (see also Kinder Scout)

CHINESE WALL GR.099891
A long way from China but this rocky crag is quite easily located along Seal Edge, where you can frequently see rock climbers scaling it. From atop this escarpment you can take in some very fine views over the Woodlands Valley.

CHINLEY (see Kinder Parishes)

CHUNNAL MOOR (1843) GR.045905
AND HARRY HUT GR.045906
A very desolate moor which is situated north west from Mill Hill, or easily reached from the Grouse Inn on the A624. Situated in the middle of this moor is an O.S. pillar called Harry Hut. Looking across the moor to the Scout it seems a long way off, and though it is not, it is one hard walk. There is only one narrow path across here so be wary of

straying in this barren tract in misty weather.

CHYNDER (see Kinder Scout)
CINDWR SOWD (see Kinder Downfall)
CISTERCIAN ABBOTS (see Edale Cross)
CLIFF OF THE BEACON FIRES (see Chendre)
CLOUGH END (see Lady Clough)

CLOUGH FARM GR.146866
A small farm holding near to the boundary of open access, midway between Edale village and Edale End. You may pass round by the rear of the house if you are making for Jaggers Clough or the Ladybower reservoir via the base of Nether Moor.

CLUTHER ROCKS (1840) GR.078875
This is an extremely rocky place which is very easily located for it lies between and below the summits of Kinder Low and the Red Brook. Children will find this a veritable playground providing they are very careful. Weatherwise, the rocks provide plenty of shelter if it should rain.

Many years ago a thriving small business was established here; a millstone quarry, whilst not too far off was to be found a smithy. There are, if you look carefully, a number of millstones to be seen, all of which are in good condition.

COATE FIELD (see Cotefield)

COLBORNE GR.095837
Formerly Colborne (1620), Coldborne Moss (1640) and Coldbourne (1725). As you will have noticed after a couple of name changes Colborne has reverted back to its original name of 1620. Colborne does not fall in the boundary of open access, however the N.T. has acquired a large tract of the terrain so you are free to wander within reason. Surprisingly, a lot of backpackers cross Colborne from Brown Knoll to Rushup Edge or vice versa not knowing that there is a railway tunnel some 800 feet (300m.) below them. This is the Cowburn Tunnel, built between 1888-1894. On Colborne you can find traces of the workings and also the navvies work village, nearly one hundred years old.

COLBORNE MOSS, COLDBOURNE (see Colborne)

COLDWELL CLOUGH AND FARM GR.056859
This is a very cold place in winter for the winds blow right down the valley to swirl around the bottom close to the farm. The clough starts its life just below Kinderlow End on Harry Moor. A brook flows the length of the clough, eventually marrying up with the River Sett at the base of the clough.

Coldwell Clough Farm lies on the ancient bridle way between Edale and Hayfield near the base of the clough. Between 1984-1986 the farm was completely renovated to bring it back to its original 17th century grandeur. The farm as it now stands is positioned on the site of the original dwelling of the medieval era. For this reason the farm was noted as a 'listed' building, and a programme was set out in 1982, starting with the barns, to bring it all back to its former glory. Until the late 1970's a 17th century sundial stood in the yard, but for some reason it was removed.

COLDWELL MOOR GR.065858
A small moor which is about ten minute's walk up from Coldwell Clough Farm, lying to the right of the old Edale to Hayfield bridle way. The moor is significant in that it lies within the acquired lands of the N.T., but does not fall within the bounds of open access. The route is waymarked across the moor into Oaken Clough then onto Southhead Farm.

CORITANI
The Coritani were the original inhabitants of the Kinder region some 2,500 years ago. They were of Celtic origin and lived mainly in the valleys, only venturing onto the high ground when danger threatened. The era they lived in was when the Kinder area was pocketed with thick forests, roamed by the wild boar and wolves. Basically the Coritani were the first livestock farmers in the High Peak living on the fringes of the forests in huts built of logs and turf.

COTEFIELD GR.132860
Formerly Coate Field (1670). This is a smallholding which lies in the Vale of Edale in the Parish of Edale, and comes within the bounds of Ollerbrook Booth. Cotefield is best viewed from the Nab on a sunny evening, for the farm looks quite serene, set in the middle of the rolling fields of the Vale. A bridle way bypasses the farm, going from Nether Booth to Edale Village.

COWBURN TUNNEL (1893) GR.074830 - 105845
The tunnel was started in 1888, but they did not start tunnelling from the ends as one might expect, but instead they sank a 900ft. shaft in the middle of Colborne. They then proceeded to work from the bottom of this shaft in two directions. However, this created problems for the tunnel frequently flooded. One serious flood reached a depth of 80ft. and whilst this was being pumped out a diving bell was brought into use for the workers to carry on driving holes into the tunnel. It was finally completed in 1893: the longest and deepest tunnel in Derbyshire, being 3702 yards (3300m.) long and 800ft. (220m.) deep. It also became the 9th longest tunnel in Britain. The odd thing about it was that there was only one air shaft. The cost of the tunnel was £270,246 - a phenomenal amount in the 1890's.

Cowburn Tunnel was officially opened in 1893 by Her Majesty Queen Victoria but it was not until the following year that it was brought into public use.

CROCKSDEN MOSSE (see Crookstone Hill)
CRODEN (see Crowden Brook/Clough)
CRODENLEE BOOTH, CRODENLIE BOOTH
(see Crowdenlee Booth)
CROEDUN (see Crowden Brook/Clough)
CROKER, TED (see Kinder Aircraft Crash Sites, R.A.F. Oxford)
CROOKSTON, CROOKSTONE BARN GR.157877
(see Crookstone Hill)

CROOKSTONE HILL GR.150880
Formerly Crocksden Mosse (1640), Crookston (1767). No crooks or stones but there is a crooked path where you can walk a crooked mile. (Pardon the pun.) This is the first hill on the north-east side of Kinder, whilst on its south eastern flanks lies the Crookstone Barn. The barn lies in between a clump of trees close to the access point of open country, again this is another barn which makes a good landmark. The access point here is very handy for people with their own transport, for this point is a long way from the nearest locality. Upon attaining the summit of the hill it is nice to turn around and reflect upon the scene behind, for now you are looking into the mouth of the Ladybower Reservoir, surrounded by the large conifer trees, reminiscent of a Norwegian fjord.

CROOKSTONE KNOLL GR.145884 AND
CROOKSTONE OUTMOOR GR.143882

The Outmoor lies on the summit of Crookstone Hill, whilst the Knoll rises up above on top of the hill and Outmoor. Though the Outmoor is nothing special, a plateau of twitching grass and boggy after a period of rain, the Knoll is rather fine. The Knoll commands a position on the Outmoor as if it was a fortress of rock, in fact from certain angles it resembles the ancient fortress of Carl Walk near Hathersage. The views from the Knoll are really magnificent and though this area is sometimes difficult to reach because of transport problems, it is worth a special effort to visit here.

CROWDEN BROOK/CLOUGH GR.103858

Formerly Crow Valley about 700 years ago, Crowdene (1550), Croden (1601), Croedun (1608). One of the largest brooks on Kinder, often crowded near its summit just below Crowden Tower by backpackers. The brook flows off the plateau near to Crowden Head cascading down into Upper Booth where it helps to form the River Noe.

A pleasant way to view the clough and brook is to follow the path up by the side of the brook from Upper Booth, the way is quite scenic though it does tend to get strenuous on the upper regions.

CROWDENE (see Crowden Brook)

CROWDEN HEAD GR.095882

A bleak bog-squelching desolate area, and not a place to be in bad weather, especially low cloud. The main Pennine Way route passes this way, but it is highly recommended not to attempt to cross this terrain without a compass bearing. The summit, though not well defined, reaches a peak of 2070ft. (631m.) the second highest point on the Scout.

CROWDENLEE BOOTH GR.103856(?)

Formerly Crodenlie Booth (1618), Crowdenley Booth (1630), Crodenlee Booth (1840). This is a lost Booth of which there is no trace remaining. Certainly there was a Booth with connections with the Crowden Brook, for there are a number of references to it in local history. The exact position of Crowdenlee is debatable, but references and old records point to it being east of the brook. Working on this assumption I would hazard at a guess that it was located on the banks of the Crowden close to a tributary coming off the western flanks of the Broadlee Bank Tor. I have based this guess on the general idea that hamlets centuries ago tended to spring up at the meeting of waters.

CROWDENLEY BOOTH (see Crowdenlee Booth)

CROWDEN TOWER (1840) GR.095871
Connected to the eastern end of the Woolpacks this jumble of rocks tower above the Crowden Brook, commanding an excellent vantage point to view the panoramic Edale Valley and the Cloughs below, especially on a bright clear sunny day.

Crowden Tower stands at the crossroads of four main routes: the first is east for Kinder Low, second west for Grindsbrook Clough, third N.N.W. for Kinder Downfall via Crowden Head along the Pennine Way and fourth, south down Crowden Brook for Upper Booth and Edale.

CROW VALLEY (see Crowdenlee Booth)
CUTLERS GREEN, CUTLERS WHEEL (see Hayfield Campsite)

—D—

DALEHEAD (1627) GR.100843
Tucked in between the small valley separating Colborne and Horsehill Tor lies a small, quaint farmhouse and outbuildings, quite picturesque in summer. The old farmhouse is surrounded by trees and has been acquired by the National Trust, who have set up a small information centre here, mainly for the summer months. There is a very small car park, for from here footpaths lead off to destinations such as Lee Estate, Upper and Barber Booth, Colborne, Horsehill Tor, Rushup Edge for Lords Seat and then onto Mam Tor. Some of these walks are an easy distance for the family out for a day's jaunt, without having to worry about getting lost, providing they stick to the signposted paths.

DAVID GRIEVE (NOVEL)
The History of David Grieve (1892) is probably the only novel ever written based on Kinder Scout. The authoress was Mrs. Humphrey Ward (1851-1920), grand-daughter of Arnold of Rugby, who wrote the novel after staying for a while at the Upper House, Hayfield. The novel is as heavy going as a Kinder bog!

DEAN HILL (1840) GR.133890
A very steep and grassy hill overlooking Blackden Barn in the pleasant Woodlands Valley. Lying off the Snake Road opposite the barn there is an access point which leads down to a footbridge across the River

Ashop, and once across here you will find yourself at the base of Dean Hill. A short walk up the hill will bring you to the main access point to open country, basically the Ashop and Blackden Moors.

DICK'S DITCH GR.058857
Formerly Dick's Sitches (1840). Lying N.W. of Southhead Farm, this ditch represents no problems for any person crossing the National Trust farmland of Southhead. The simple reason is that the main path, which you must strictly adhere to, runs atop of Dick's Ditch and is also fenced off from the public. The ditch, acquired by the N.T., has been converted into a conservation area. In years to come it is hoped that the young saplings of beech, birch, oak and ash planted by the N.T. will become a mini nature reserve for any wildlife. It is also hoped that it will create a shelter for the resident livestock.

DICK'S SITCHES (see Dick's Ditch)

DIMPUS (1840) GR.073854
Formerly Dympus. Either way it is an unusual name, but if it was not for the name this area would really be insignificant to the walker. This area lays claim to the two main tributaries that make up the start of the River Sett. Land around here is rather squelchy with the upper regions which lie below Brown Knoll becoming increasingly peaty. It is hard to imagine that centuries ago the land hereabouts was covered in alder trees.

DIMPUS CLOUGH GR.060850
Located below and between Mount Famine and South Head, just inside the open country boundary. The terrain in the clough is very mossy and grassy, but very boggy at its base after a heavy downpour. Do not talk to strange girls here for you may well be talking to a ghost. Legend says that this area is haunted by a girl dressed in white who was murdered in the 16th century. The foul deed was supposed to have been committed at the old South Head Farm, where after the murder the corpse was dragged across to the clough and the body so arranged as to look like suicide.

DIMPUS GATE GR.058847
This is in actual fact a three hundred year old packhorse route between the villages of Hayfield and Castleton via the Rushup Edge road. A small section of the route, namely between Highgate Head, Hayfield, and the S.W. base of Mount Famine, re-traces a Roman

road. Dimpus Gate Track, as it is more commonly known, passes above the haunted Dimpus Clough, and between the two picturesque hills of Mount Famine and South Head. At the base of South Head the track swings round its base between two sets of stone pillars, then continues on its merry way down to Rushup Edge and on to Castleton.

DOCTOR'S ROAD GR.045870
A long lost road which ran from Jumble Lane, Hayfield, over the top of Kinder Bank, then dropping down to exit near Bowden Bridge. It is also believed that this long lost road was the original Roman road to Kinder, for Roman coins were found along here many years ago.

DOWNFALL (see Kinder Downfall)
DRINKWATER, WILL (see Edale Cross)
DRUIDS' ALTAR (see Nether Moor)

DRUIDS' STONE GR.135874
Folklore has it that the ancient Druids used to hold counsel here, this can be borne out through the fact that close by on Nether Moor there was a Druids' altar. The rock is the largest amongst a jumble of small ones located on the high edge of Rowland Cote Moor, where the footpath can be traced right beside it. On the top of the stone there are to be found a number of indentations, these are due to weather erosion, and not as many people think, notches hued out by the Druids' fires.

The views from here are magificent taking in the Blue John Mine, The Great Ridge, Winnats Pass, Vale of Edale, The Hope Valley, Ladybower Reservoir and the Ashopton Viaduct.

DRY CLOUGH GR.119875
Formerly Dry Clough House (1850), for there used to be a smallholding at the base of the clough, though no trace is visible of this house now. As the name implies, this is a semi-dry clough running down in the shadows of the towering Nether Tor. When the clough is flowing with water it helps to swell the Grinds Brook. The summit of the clough marks the point of the Seven Minute Crossing, where you can cross the summit of Kinder in about seven minutes.

DRY CLOUGH HOUSE (see Dry Clough)

DUNGE CLOUGH (1840) GR.124895
Another place found in the Woodlands Valley, sandwiched between

The Wicken and Wood Moor. This small clough has a brook which feeds the River Ashop below, whilst the clough itself has steep flanks on either side. Along one side of the clough many years ago grew an abundance of trees; alas none are to be seen now.

DYMPUS (see Dimpus)

—E—

ECHOING ROCKS (see Ringing Roger)

EDALE GR.125855
Formerly Ae - dael an Anglo Saxon name meaning 'Valley of the river' or 'Valley of the running stream'. It is next mentioned in the Domesday Book as Ai - Edale this was in 1086, two hundred years later we have Heydale in 1251 and Ei - Eydale in 1280. In 1550 we find that it has changed in its pronunciation with the dropping of the 'Dale' for now it has become Edall. Edale itself refers to the whole valley between the Kinder escarpments and the opposite ridge more commonly known these days as 'The Great Ridge'. However, with the coming of the railway the village of Grindsbrook is more commonly referred to as Edale village.

The village lies about a ten minute walk up the road from the station and the car park opposite.

Edale is the starting point of the Pennine Way, behind the Old Nag's Head Inn. The village boasts two inns, a church, and a campsite shop. The church is the Holy Trinity, built in 1885. Across the road from the church lies the original cemetery dating back to the 16th century, which is worth a stroll around looking at the ancestoral locals. Also to be found in this cemetery is an ancient sundial. Prior to this cemetery the Edale deceased were buried in Castleton. They were literally carried over the Great Ridge via Hollins Cross on the route which was termed 'The Coffin Track'.

Though the village is very busy at the weekends, especially in summer, this does not detract from the fact that its location is in an idyllic setting. Services available close to the village include the National Park Information Centre, Peak District Warden Service and the area's Mountain Rescue Post. (see Section 5)

EDALE CROSS GR.078861
Formerly Edowe Cross. This is an old medieval stone cross standing on the packhorse route between Hayfield and Edale. Records seem to

indicate that the erection of the cross was done by the Cistercian Abbots of Besingweal Abbey, Holywell, North Wales, to mark the boundary of the land owned by them. After standing against the elements for several centuries it eventually fell over, where it remained until 1810 whence along came a gentleman by the name of Thomas Gee, a local farmer of the Ashes Farm, Hayfield. After careful consideration he decided to re-erect the cross, so off he went to seek out some help. Four men, George and Joseph Hadfield, residents of Upper Booth, John Shirt of Lee Farm and Will Drinkwater from the now derelict Hollins Head Farm offered their services. After some huffing and puffing they had the cross standing erect again, where they then made it secure. This done they decided that they must carve out their initials upon the cross for posterity. They have often been criticized for defacing an ancient monument, but remember in those days there were no laws protecting ancient monuments. Thomas Gee's initials stand out the most along with the year. The cross is now protected under the Ancient Monuments Acts.

EDALE END GR.163364
Formerly Edowe Heade (1640). Edale End is exactly what the name implies, the end of Edale, the border of the Parishes of Edale and Hope. It lies some three miles (4kms.) from Edale station. The place is made up of a few small farm dwellings and their outbuildings, of which one house belongs to the Peak Planning Board. The main access point for crossing over to the Ladybower Reservoir and the Dams via Hope Cross lies through this small quaint place.

EDALE FLYER
Not as you might expect, a person flying around in a plane or hang gliding over Edale, but a name given to a steam train of an era now gone. Every Sunday morning, about 8.30a.m., there used to be a steam train which left the now defunct Manchester Central station, bound for Sheffield. The train was usually full to capacity, but upon arrival at Edale seventy five per cent of the passengers would alight. Hence the name. Time travels on but not the steam train. No more can be heard the shrill whistle as the 'Flyer' thunders out of the Cowburn tunnel into the Vale of Edale.

EDALE HEAD GR.085868
Edale Head is often confused with its neighbour, The Cloughs, the simple reason being that they both connect with each other. The Head is situated on the upper slopes of the southern region of Kinder;

basically the area round the Noe Stool. Edale Head refers to the start of the River Edale just below the Noe Stool. Peat abounds in this area making it very boggy in wet weather.

EDALE HEAD HOUSE GR.088860

Why the house was so named is a mystery to me, for it is nowhere near Edale Head! In fact, the house stood on the opposite hill, not even overlooking Edale Head. This house, not far from Jacob's Ladder, was the residence of the 'bragging man' Jacob Marshall, after whom Jacob's Ladder was named. Though the house is now in ruins you will find it very handy as a wind break or as a shelter, in the lee of one of the walls, in wet weather. But be warned! this house was reputed to be haunted!

(Bragging, a term used in the 18th century for the art of buying and selling.)

EDALE MILL GR.134854

Originally built in the 18th century as a tannery and subsequently powered by the fast flowing River Noe. After the demise of the small tannery industry it was rebuilt in 1795 then used as a lace thread spinning mill. The women who worked here and lived at Castleton often stayed and slept the night if the weather was too bad to make the long journey back to Castleton. The mill ceased to be viable in 1934 so it was only used for storage.

EDALE MOOR GR.095872

This moor is another barren area made up of a compilation of minor rocks and a few thousand tons of sodden peat. It is also the start of the wild Kinder Plateau on its southern side lying between the Grindslow Knoll and the towering Crowden Tower. The Plateau sees the start of the meandering Crowden Brook before it starts on its cascading journey down into the Vale of Edale.

EDALE ROAD (see Over Horse Waie)

EDALE ROCKS (1840) GR.079867

Standing majestically and commanding a panoramic view, these rocks seem to rise out of the ground as if they were the crown atop of Kinder Scout's head. They stand on the Pennine Way alternative route and act as an extremely good landmark. If you look at the rocks head-on they seem very hard to climb, but nothing is further from the truth, for the back of the rocks slope down to meet the Plateau making a gentle way up to their summit. On attaining the summit you may look out in a 360 degree sweep and take in some of the finest views of Kinder and the surrounding moors.

EDALE STATION GR.123854
The station is conveniently situated near the T junction of the main thoroughfare in the Vale of Edale. The station is very basic consisting of two concrete platforms and two concrete bus-style open shelters; a far cry from when the station was first built. For then it had two long wooden platforms, a ticket office-cum-station-master's-office and two large wooden waiting rooms. There was usually a staff of about four -now there is none.

EDALL (see Edale)
EDOWE CROSS (see Edale Cross)
EDOWE HEAD (see Edale End)

EGG CRAG GR.096897
Happiness is egg shaped so the old television jingle went and, happiness in this case is this crag, suitable for rock climbers of varying skills. The location of this fine crag (which resembles Edale Rocks) is on the eastern edges of the Fairbrook Naze. A veritable playground for rock climbers.

EI - EYDLAE (see Edale)
ELLE BANK, ELLERS BANK (see Hayfield Campsite)
ESSOPE (see River Ashop)
EYDALE (see Edale)

—F—

FAIR BROOK AND FAIRBROOK WATERFALL GR.093892
Formerly The Farre Brook (1627). A very long and almost straight brook that starts its life on the Kinder Plateau, from where it then makes its way flowing between the escarpments of the Fairbrook Naze and Seal Edge. On the O.S. map there is a waterfall shown near to the brook's summit, but if you expect to find a gushing torrent you will be in for a surprise. It is only the brook cascading over some rocks on its downward journey to marry up with the River Ashop below. Indeed if the summer has been a rather dry one then the brook becomes but a trickle, if not drying up altogether. A good aspect of the brook is that you can follow it down to the Snake Road, exiting near the Snake Inn where you may take some refreshment before continuing your way.

FAIRBROOK NAZE GR.096898

Formerly The Faire Brook Edge (1627). The Naze or Nose as it is often called is the far northern escarpment of the Kinder Edge, the summit reaching 2049 feet (625m). It is a very rocky region where you may watch rock climbers partaking in their favourite pastime. I have spent many a happy and contented hour here contemplating the wonderful scenery below and the opposite moors. Another beauty of the place is that there are plenty of windbreaks and shelter in inclement weather.

FAIRVAGE CLOUGH (see Bray Clough)

FARLANDS HOUSE/LODGE AND BOOTH GR.053877

These two buildings more or less make up a small community, with Booth Farm commanding a small ridge on which it has stood in its present form for close on 260 years, unlike Farlands which has not long passed its centenary. Booth Farm, formerly Bothe (1580), is typical in structure of the period in which it was built. The farmhouse is stone with the farmyard itself being cobbled; around the yard are a couple of barns. Access through the farmyard is allowed to gain Hills House, The Ashes and Coldwell Clough. There has been some sort of a farming community here since the medieval period, but Bothe, as it was called, did not really start to flourish until the farmhouse-cum-cottages were built in the early part of the 17th century.

Farlands House and the lodge opposite which lies between Booth and the main house were built in the latter part of the 18th century. The main house was built in 1867 on the main bridleway of the time to Upper House and beyond. Farlands was acquired by a Mr. James Watt, a gentleman of some standing, who lived and owned Abney Hall, Cheadle near Stockport. He acquired this fine house as a country retreat. In 1917 he let the main house to a Mr. and Mrs. Knot; she outlived her husband and spent some 50 years living here. The latter part of her tenancy saw the house fall into an abysmal state of decay. After her demise the grandson of James Watt, Matthew, along with George and Eva Hodgson, set about restoring and modernising the house, until once again Farlands looks quite impressive.

FAR UPPER TOR GR.110876

One of the three towering tors that command positions overlooking the picturesque Grindsbrook Clough. This tor looks directly over and across at the Grindslow Knoll, but unlike its two sisters this tor is not as widely used for rock climbing.

FEATHERBED MOSS (1843) GR.085925

I could use some really strong words to describe this terrain! This barren moor across which the Pennine Way passes from Kinder to Bleaklow is nearly as bad as crossing the Kinder Plateau. At least when you are crossing the Plateau you expect the worse, but here? Even on a dry spell it can be a sea of squelchy mud and peat, so you can imagine what it is like after some rain. It is strongly advised to cross the moss on or as close to the Pennine Way route as possible, and always have your compass handy, for mists are quite common. I have been caught here in a mist on a very bad rainy day and I can tell you I was glad of my compass.

FEATHERBED TOP (1850) GR.090921/
SALVIN RIDGE GR.096920

Both these areas hold the same terrain as Featherbed Moss, so the less said the better. Featherbed Top is the summit of the Featherbed Moss, attaining a height of 1785ft. (544m). Salvin Ridge, another mound, connects with the Featherbed Top, which make distinguishing them apart very hard. This confuses some people as to which is the highest point, though there is very little in it.

FIELDHEAD (1774) GR.125857

Before the Information Centre was built this area was farmland belonging to Fieldhead Farm, no longer with us. Fieldhead was so named because years ago this was the first and foremost field of this area, an apt position for the centre. Instead of grazing and crop land as it used to be, the only items planted here now are tent pegs, for it has now become a camping area.

FIELDHEAD INFORMATION CENTRE GR.124856

Located about halfway up the Edale village road this National Park centre is well worth a visit. An enjoyable hour may be spent in here for there is much to see, including a slide show. This centre also houses the area's Mountain Rescue Kit and Post.

FOG FIELD WELL GR.056861

An old well that was located in the middle of the field where the path runs from the Ashes Farm to Coldwell Clough Farm. Locals swore that it was the sweetest water for miles. Perhaps there was some truth in this, for it was known that a certain gentleman made a yearly pilgrimage from Manchester to drink of this water!

FOUR JACKS CABIN GR.104879

Formerly Micah's Church. The remains of this stone cabin may be located near the source of the Grinds Brook, out on Wove Hill, Kinder Plateau. This cabin was the highest in the Peak District and was built by Mike Tym, a devout methodist, whose profession was game-keeper for a local Edale family. It was through his association with the methodist church that the cabin became known as Micah's Church. The cabin eventually fell into disrepair, but it was still required as a shooting cabin. So along came four men who just happened to all have the same christian name of Jack. These four totally rebuilt the cabin and at the same time extended it a bit - hence the Four Jacks Cabin. It must have been a lonely place out there on the bleak Plateau, especially in bad weather, though its position seems justified on a bend on the banks of the brook. Only the foundations remain today and little of these are to be seen.

FOX HOLES GR.108871

Plenty of holes but I have not seen any foxes, though I presume this place was named after the lairs of the fox all those years ago. It is an extremely rock strew area which lies directly beneath the Grindslow Knoll, but overlooks the Grindsbrook Clough.

—G—

GARSIDE, LUKE (1841-1913)

Garside was a member of the Northern Counties and Peak District Footpaths Preservation Society in the late 19th century. He was a native of Hayfield and was reputed to know everything on the subject of his village. With his influence and the backing of the NCPDFPS they managed to create a right-of-way between Hayfield and the Snake Inn, the Snake Path.

In 1880 he had a book published called *Kinder Scout, the Footpaths and Bridle Roads* - a fascinating book to read for much of the land and especially the paths have long since altered or disappeared. It also gives a very detailed insight to the Scout on the Hayfield side, as well as the surrounding moors. The book has been re-published in a handy pocket size and is highly recommended.

GATE SIDE CLOUGH GR.118898

Centuries ago a well trodden path followed the course of this small clough; the faint path visible now is not the original. The clough has a number of tributaries, all of which run down off the Seal Flats. The base of the clough is fairly stony whilst part of the clough becomes somewhat rocky. About a third of the way up the clough can be found the ruins of a shooting cabin; one of many found scattered around the moors of Kinder.

GEE BANKS GR.052858
A moor of access and no access, the summit being the boundary. The land facing Kinder from the summit of this small moor falls within the access area whilst the land behind, facing Ollerset Moor, has no access, excepting for a small path you may use to gain access to the Kinder Estate. Gee Banks facing the Ashes Farm is known to the locals as either Gee Bones or Gee Bongs, which seemed to originate from some previous tenants of the Ashes Farm who had their ashes scattered over the area which overlooked the farm. Of the no access area, this is made up of the grazing lands of three farms: Stubbs, Rowan and Higher Heys. Close to these farms run the old roman road which connected Glossop with Brough (Hope). From off this ancient road, to the left of the base of Mount Famine, can be located another access path to the Kinder Estate. Both of these paths (the other being via Higher Heys Farm), require you to keep to them until open country is gained.

A good vantage point is attained by following the Mount Famine access path then turning to your left and keeping to the wall until you reach a small rocky crag. The view is not as spectacular as from the summit of Mount Famine itself.

GEE BONES, GEE BONGS (see Gee Banks)

GEE, JOHN THOMAS (1844-1921)
A resident of the Ashes Farm and a well respected character of Hayfield. He was a member and organiser of many of Hayfield's committees and fêtes etc. However, it is the Harry Moor water storage tanks that lie beneath the moor that he is remembered for most. He had the forethought to tap and collect this pure water which continuously flows down underground from the Scout. There is close to 500,000 gallons of water in these tanks under Harry Moor, which supply all the districts around Hayfield.

GEE, THOMAS (see Edale Cross)

GHOSTS AND APPARITIONS
Most country villages in Britain have at least one spook in the locality,

and so does Kinder and the surrounding countryside. The following seven places have either had sightings or there has been an eerie atmosphere about the place. All seven have been mentioned under their relevant text, the seven are:- Mill Hill, (Liberator crash site), Stones House, Dimpus Clough, Hope Brink, Terror Bridge, The Tips Haunting and Edale Head House. Happy hauntings....

GLEAD HILL (1850) GR.074915/MOSS CASTLE GR.072916
Do not look for a castle in this godforsaken place, for the name refers to a hilly landmass of moss and peat. Both the Moss and Glead Hill are situated on the Pennine Way between Mill Hill and the barren land of the Featherbed Moss. However, to take in Moss Castle you have to take a very small detour, marked out by poles and stakes which meet up at Glead Hill. Do not rely on these poles for as with the Featherbed Moss, this area is suspect to sudden mists. Glead Hill is topped by a small stump in the middle of a thick peat bog - the last marker before crossing the Featherbed to the Snake Pass Summit. A compass is essential over this terrain.

GOLDEN CLOUGH (1840) GR.122870
A meandering clough that has a very pleasant cascading brook flowing the length of it. The brook commences its merry journey from off the Plateau between Blackden Edge and Nether Tor, tumbling down in the shadow of the scenic Ringing Roger, eventually taking its marital vows with the Grinds Brook. This is the point of open access and though the clough is very pleasant to view it is rather steep to climb - but it is possible.

GRAIN CLOUGH GR.093854
Boundary clough for both open access and National Trust land. The clough separates Brown Knoll and the Horsehill Tor, becoming very steep near to the summit. Lee Estate Farm and cottages face the foot of the old clough, where it is slightly wooded.

GREAT BUTTRESS GR.082888
This buttress lies in the magnificent amphitheatre of the Kinder Downfall opposite the Kinder Buttress. Both are playgounds for rock climbers, especially the Great Buttress.

GREAT HAMMEL, GREAT HAMLET (see Hayfield)

GREAT HEYFIELD (1637)
Four hundred years ago Little Hayfield and Hayfield, separate communities within themselves were incorporated to make Great Heyfield. Bureaucracy being what it was and still is in certain cases, this was deemed a sensible move, combining the two. It did not suit the locals though, for they preferred to have their own little separate hamlets. By 1640 they had managed to get their own way with Little Hayfield becoming Little Heyfield and Hayfield becoming Great Hamlet.

GRIMESBROOKE, GRIMSBROK BOTH, GRINDS BOOTH
(see Grindsbrook Booth)

GRINDS BROOK AND GRINDSBROOK CLOUGH
(1840) GR.115874
The Grinds Brook is a meandering brook flowing off the Plateau down through the pleasant and panoramic Grindsbrook Clough. It passes through the charming Grindsbrook Booth (Edale village) then behind Fieldhead Information Centre, to flow under Yemans Bridge before it meets the River Noe. The start and first stretch of the long Pennine Way passes through Grindsbrook Clough. In winter the path through the clough can become dangerous for quite often water on the path and on the stones and rocks freezes making walking very hazardous. Do not let this deter you because the winter views in the clough can be quite breathtaking - just be wary where you put your feet!

GRINDSBROOK BOOTH (1840) GR.123860
Formerly Grymesbroke (1342), Grimsbruk Both (1561), Grimesbrooke (1607), Grymesbrook Booth (1608) and Grinds Booth (1767). As you will have noticed, this booth has led a varied existence in both pronunciation and spelling in its life span. Nowadays it is more commonly referred to as Edale village. It has over the years become more famous as the official starting point of the Pennine Way. The start of this most famous of all long walks in Britain lies just behind the Old Nags Head Inn, across an erected log footbridge fording the Grinds Brook. (see Edale)

GRINDSBROOK TOWERS GR.107875
Nothing like Blackpool Tower! In fact they are not like towers at all, for they represent two large rocky escarpments. These are likened to sentinels either side of the Grinds Brook as it flows off the Plateau at the right-hand fork of the Grindsbrook Clough Head. After heavy rain

the brook fairly gushes between these two escarpments, which means a slight detour when fording the brook at the summit of the towers. If semi-dry, which it often is, there is no problem for there are a number of fording points across these rocks.

GRINDSLOW HOUSE GR.133864
A smallholding on the banks of the Grinds Brook just past the start of the Pennine Way. You do not have to worry about crossing their land for it is out of bounds.

GRINDSLOW KNOLL (1840) GR.110869
Believe it or not, but this is quite a skiing resort in the snow-bound winter months; whilst in the summer from its summit you can take in some splendid views. The Knoll refers to a small pinnacle which tops the hill, and atop of the pinnacle there is a large cairn of stones. The summit of Grindslow Knoll is somewhat rocky but this does not present any problems for the walker.

GROUSE INN GR.034905
A public house on the Hayfield to Glossop road, A624. This inn makes either a good starting or finishing point for the crossing of Burnt Hill on to Mill Hill. Excellent snacks at reasonable prices can be obtained here.

—H—

HADFIELD, GEORGE AND JOSEPH (see Edale Cross)
HALDENCLUGH (see Holden Clough)
HALIFAX, HAMPDEN BOMBER AND HANDLEY PAGE, HEYFORD (see Kinder Aircraft Crash Sites)
HARRY HUT (see Chunnal Moor)

HARRY MOOR (1840) GR.062863
Harry Moor sits below Kinderlow End just outside the boundary of open access, but within the boundary of the National Trust. If you happen to ramble across this moor, just think that below your feet there is literally thousands of gallons of water stored in tanks. (see Gee, John Thomas)

The main path to gain access to the moor from Hayfield is via Tunstead Clough Farm and its surrounding grazing fields. So when crossing this land please respect it and keep to all the paths way-marked for you.

HARTS HORN GR.112879

With a summit of 1960ft. (597m) this hill, part of the Kinder Plateau, represents another of those barren places found on Kinder. The Horn is capped by a couple of large boulders making it a very good landmark in clear weather when you are trekking within the Blackden Rind vicinity. A fine view can be had from here of the land leading up to the summit of the Grindsbrook Towers, whilst a short walk will bring you out onto the rocky escarpment of Upper Tor above Grindsbrook Clough.

HAYFIELD GR.040868

Roughly translated it means, heathy open land. Former names are Hedfelt (1086), Heyfeld (1285), Heathfield (1577), Great Hamell (1625), Great Hamlet (1640). (Also see Great Heyfield)

The village stands on the River Sett which in the year 1748 burst its banks causing widespread damage, especially to the churchyard where it literally ripped the cadavers out of their graves.

Hayfield is the main access point for Kinder on the western side, with many paths leading out from the village to various points of entry onto Kinder. There is a small information centre on the site of the old railway station. The line closed in the 1960's and it was later decided to take the rails up all the way back to New Mills. A nature trail was born, the Sett Valley Trail, which is a pleasant walk of three miles (5km.) starting from the information centre.

HAYFIELD CAMPSITE GR.048868/ELLE BANK GR.048866

The campsite is quite large and there is ample room for vehicles. The access point for vehicles lies opposite the Bowden Bridge quarry. For the person on foot there is a pleasant ten minute walk from Hayfield village along the banks of the River Sett. At the site there is a small camp shop which also houses a ranger post, where at weekends can be found a weather information chart for the area. Campers wishing to pitch their tents or caravanettes are well advised to book in advance if possible to avoid disappointment. The camp is usually closed from November to April.

Encroaching onto the campsite and by the side of Stones House is a thickly wooded area, Elle Bank, formerly Elle or Ellers Bank. Access can be gained from one or two locations for there is a path running through the wood as also there is one running around the perimeter. This wood covered the site of the camping area centuries ago, but the trees were cut back to lay bare a small green belt formerly called Cutler's Green or Cutler's Wheel. It is rumoured that cutlery was made here more than two hundred years ago. Before the campsite was created there stood here Kinder Printworks, built in the last century.

HAYFIELD FLOODS

There have been several floods in Hayfield's existence, some of which were serious. Four of the floods are mentioned here. July 1748, was probably the worst, for the River Sett burst its banks creating a devastation beyond belief in such a small community. Cottages and outbuildings were flooded, two people were drowned, numerous people were injured, water mills were swept aside, but the most shocking scene was the churchyard. The river in its torrential flood literally tore up the graves causing coffins and bodies to be strewn about Hayfield. This must have been a terrible sight to the locals, especially to any relatives of the departed.

August 1799 saw the Sett rise again. This time it carried off the main bridge in Hayfield as well as claiming more life.

In 1809 the River Sett once again caused havoc by washing away a number of buildings which included a bakehouse and a bakers .

June 1858 saw torrential rain flood the River Kinder on the Scout resulting in the Downfall gushing forth a devastating torrent upon the valley below. More cottages and a mill weir were torn up and washed away in the ensuing flood.

These days it is a more sedate and serene life in the Hayfield valley, but who knows when the wrath of the river will be let loose again?

HAYFIELD MOOR (see Middle and Upper Moor)

HEARDMAN, FRED (1896-1973)

Bill the Bog Trotter, this was the nickname of Fred Heardman, probably Kinder's very own walking encyclopaedia. A celebrated hill-walker, he was also host at the *Old Nag's Head*, Edale. He formerly lived at Tunstead House. In 1922 he made the first double Marsden -Edale walk. Once he walked from Langsett to Edale for the wager of a pint of shandy! A local councillor, he opposed the industrialization of the Edale valley with success. The *Nag's Head* was the first Information Office and Mountain Rescue post of the new National Park.

HEATHFIELD (see Hayfield)

HEATHFIELD CHAPEL GR.050870?

An 11th century chapel reputedly the first in Hayfield. It probably stood at the water-meetings of the Sett and Kinder where Bowden Bridge now stands.

HEDFELT (see Hayfield)
HEGATE, HEGHATE (see Highgate)

HERON ROCK/STONE GR.049870
A large prominent rock which stands majestically at the end of Oldpits Plantation above a quarry and facing the holdings of Farlands and Booth. The ashes of a certain Mrs. Johnson whose husband served Mr. James and Jack Watts of Farlands and Upper House were scattered over this proud rock, overlooking Farland Lodge where she had resided. If you are travelling in any direction along the Snake Path across Middle Moor, make it a point to divert at the old white shooting cabin for this rock, it is only a five minute walk away and you will not be disappointed. When I have been walking over Kinder and have a couple of hours to spare, then this is where I make for. A person can spend a pleasant hour or two here in tranquil solitude. You overlook the Kinder Amphitheatre and the farmlands of Booth, Hills House, The Ashes and Coldwell... No matter what time of the year it is, the valley below and the land beyond are quite serene and picturesque.

HEYDALE (see Edale)
HEYFELDCLYF (see Kinder Head)
HEYFIELD MOOR (see Middle and Upper Moor)
HIGHER HOUSE (see Upper House)

HIGHGATE GR.045860
Formerly Heghgate (1381) and Hegate (1468). An old road that takes you up out of Hayfield on a stiff climb to within the shadow of Mount Famine. It is in this vicinity where it was part of an old roman road and it connects here with the ancient Dimpus Gate Track for Castleton. In a severe winter, this road is impassable for snow drifts tend to get trapped between the two dry stone walls with the depth of the snow reaching well above the average person's head.

HIGHMOOR PITS (see Black Moor)
HILLS HOUSE, HAYFIELD (see Peep o' Day)

HILL'S HOUSE, HAYFIELD/
HILL HOUSE FARM, HAYFIELD GR.052871
Hill's House was built in 1723 by Samuel Marriott, whose grandfather

in 1536 had a small dwelling nearby, aptly called, Marriott's Place. For the next 375 years the descending Marriotts lived on this land. The downfall of the Marriotts came by way of the building of the Kinder Reservoir, for part of the land was used for the railway to the workings and also some of the land was taken up by the navvies' huts. The last Marriott, Samuel, who it seems was quite a 'Jack the lad' and very fond of a tipple or two, never claimed any compensation for the use of his land and this consequently led him into bankruptcy. About 1909 the farm was sold off.

Across the way from Hill's House is Hill House Farm. Little is known about the early existence of this old stone farmhouse. We know it dates back to the late 17th century, but the land barely yielded enough to feed and clothe the farmer and his family, so by the late 19th century the farm had run down considerably. Thirty years were to pass before Harold and Mary Hodgson took over and sank their life savings into the farm - £100. Over the years the Hodgsons rebuilt the farm and land, gradually gaining the largest sheep farm for miles around. Harold lived for 46 years at the farm before dying in 1973; still doing a full day's work.

HODGSON, EVA AND GEORGE (see Farlands)
HODGSON, GEORGE AND MARY
(see Hill House Farm, Hayfield)

HOLDEN CLOUGH (1817) GR.073928
Formerly Haldenclugh (1290). This is one of the most charming cloughs I have come across, especially so in spring during the lambing season. The clough starts about twenty minutes walk down the Snake Road from the Snake Pass summit in the direction of Glossop. The start is a little bit rocky with a brook flowing through the length of it into Hurst Reservoir at Glossop. About a third of the way through the clough opens out into a large basin, then continues on the other side in a narrow defile. The basin in spring is usually full of sheep and lambs, and often I have sat here admiring the serenity.

Half way through the clough it finds itself some company, being bounded on one side by Span Moor whilst on the other side it has the company of Ramsley Moor.

HOLLINGWORTH CLOUGH GR.045896
Formerly Hollingworth Clough Head. No recognised path through this clough which is to be found between Burnt Hill and Leygathead Moor. However, this clough can be trekked through by following the

brook up from Carr Meadow to Mill Hill or vice versa. You will find the going very hard for the brook has to be criss-crossed several times. If attempting the walk from Carr Meadow then the terrain tends to get tougher the higher you go. The walk is about 2 miles (3kms.) long, but it seems never ending and is only recommended for the hardy walker.

HOLLINGWORTH CLOUGH HEAD (see Hollingworth Clough)

HOLLINGWORTH WATERFALL GR.046898

The waterfall is located about a mile or so (2kms.) along the Hollingworth Clough from the direction of the Carr Meadow footbridge. It is not as grand as Kinder Downfall neither is it as spectacular, but it does hold a certain charm of its own. The height of the waterfall is about 21ft. (7m) high, and is quite enchanting in the summer sunshine, it looks so inviting. If by chance you are walking the length of Hollingworth Clough then this is an ideal place to rest and have some nourishment.

HOLLIN HEAD AND
HOLLINSHEAD FARM REMAINS GR.065886

Lying on the north-eastern flanks of the Kinder Reservoir this hump has to be crossed or skirted around to gain access to the Peter Nook Wood and its pleasant little valley. There is a small clough which cuts through the hump called Hollin Head, together with a small brook which a hundred years ago was called the Spar or Spaw. It seems another part of Kinder's heritage has disappeared unless people start to refer to the brook as the Spar or Spaw again.

Situated on the banks of the Spaw are to be found the remains of a once thriving farm. Alas, with the building of the reservoir all that changed. All that remains today are a couple of small depleted walls.

HOPE (see Kinder Parishes)

HOPE BRINK GR.175853

Formerly Brink in 1848. A small ridge lying below the first or last ridge of the Kinder Massif, Thornhill Brink. Hope Brink once formed part of a roman road which linked the roman forts of Melandra at Glossop and Anavio at Brough. There is a legend that says the path is haunted by the spirits of a roman legion, forever marching along this ridge. You have been warned!

HOPE CROSS GR.161857

Less of a cross, more of a pillar in stature. This ancient monument which has inscribed upon it the year 1137 stands on the old roman road of the Hope Brink. As regards to the year inscribed upon it, take no notice, for this monument is far older than the inscription. Once again this is another piece of Kinder's heritage that makes a very good landmark.

HOPE WOODLANDS, HOPPA AND HOPPE (see Kinder Parishes)

HORSEHILL TOR (1840) AND TAGS NAZE GR.093848

Tags Naze refers to a large cleft on the eastern flanks of the tor which overlooks the farm called The Orchards. Horsehill Tor has become quite a headache at times for walkers, for there are so many boundaries here. There are the open access and the National Trust boundaries which includes a small area closed to the public at certain times. Tread warily here, though in general, providing all walkers and the general public take heed of the country and mountain codes, it is more than likely that nothing will be said or done. There are some very fine views from the summit as well as a couple of items of interest. On the summit there can be located an old boundary stone, close by this stone in an easterly direction you should come across the fragments of a crashed Thunderbolt aircraft. Happy hunting.

HURST MOOR (see Span Moor and Clough)

—J—

JACOBS LADDER GR.087864

There are times when I wish this was a ladder, for at least it would be a lot easier in climbing to the top of this very steep hill! The ladder refers to a path which starts at an old packhorse bridge and meanders upwards round a hill overlooking the cloughs. Although now almost eroded with the passing of time, the original steps were cut into the hillside by Jacob Marshall, resident of Edale Head House in the 17th century. For reasons known only to himself, he was rather fond of clambering up this steep meandering hill the hard way, instead of the much easier packhorse route left of the ladder. At the base and summit of the ladder are notices warning of danger; please take note. The packhorse bridge at the base of the ladder, commonly known as Yongate, has undergone extensive repairs over the years, and utilising the original stone has returned it to its original format. The only exception being the struts now giving extra support to the bridge.

JAGGERS CLOUGH (1815) GR.145878
Formerly Jaggers Gate in 1688. The clough is about two miles (4 kms.) long with a pleasant brook meandering through the length of it. On both sides of the clough it is bounded by the Upper and Nether Moors and Crookstone Hill and Moor. The upper regions of this clough become somewhat rocky and very hard going, offsett by the small cascading waterfalls and the scenic view down through the clough and the moors beyond.

Centuries ago the lower regions were used as a packhorse route by men called 'Jaggers', who together with their horses toted their packs along this route. We cannot be certain as to what they carried, however there is a slight inclination that it may have been ore, for it is known that Castleton was rich in lead. It is not known exactly when this particular clough was first used regularly for transportation, but we do know that it was extensively used in the 17th century.

JAGGERS GATE (see Jaggers Clough)
JOHNSON MRS. (see Heron Rock)
JUBILEE TRAIL (see Stephenson, Tom)

—K—

KINDER AMPHITHEATRE GR.070885
The Amphitheatre is generally named as the area which starts at the Kinder Downfall, falling down to the Peter Nook area then widening out to take in its boundaries of Hollin Head and its opposite counterpart of Blackshaws. From here it now widens out to its widest points at William Clough at its northern end and Kinder Head at its southern proximity, culminating at the dam wall of the Kinder Reservoir.

For the best place to view the Amphitheatre, I suggest that you make a pilgrimage to the escarpment of Heron Rock.

KINDER BANK GR.047868
Formerly Kynder Banke in 1346. This bank is open all day and everyday for investors who like to gain a little interest in the splendid views of the western edges of Kinder and also the reservoir. The banking is on the left-hand side of the road leading up to the Kinder Reservoir, it mainly consists of trees with the odd quarry here and there. Paths run along the top and there is also one through the wood.

KINDER BROOCKE (see River Kinder)

KINDER BUTTRESS GR.078889
A buttress in the Kinder Downfall amphitheatre, perhaps not quite as famous as its counterpart, the Great Buttress. Below lie rocks jutting out at all angles, so one slip can cause quite an accident - care needed!

KINDER CAVERN (1840) GR.073867
Legend or myth? True or false? Hundreds, nae thousands, have searched in vain for this infamous cavern, becoming convinced that it is just part of old folklore. However, it does exist, but you will be disappointed if you expect something on the scale of one of the Castleton caves. It is only a small opening which is located between some rocks, just a few yards from the Kinder Low tumulus in a westerly direction.

KINDER COTTAGE (see Kinders of Kinder)

KINDER DOWNFALL GR.082869
Formerly *Cindwr Scwd* which found its origin in the Celtic language, *Kinder Scut,* a Saxon name meaning 'water over the edge' and Downfall in 1840. 'All roads lead to Rome', so they say, well as regards to Kinder 'all roads lead to the Downfall'. The Downfall is a large cleft cut into the rock face and made up of a jumble of rocks which have over the centuries broken away from this face to lay strewn about at the base of the waterfall. Over the summit flows the River Kinder, though at this point it is only a brook. It cascades over the top to drop about 100ft. (30m) into the valley below then on to feed the Kinder Reservoir.

Two features of the Downfall worth waiting to see: the unusual sight of the waterfall being whipped back up the face of the Downfall creating a huge fountain of spray sometimes as high as 50ft. (15m) above the lip of the Downfall. This can be seen miles away on a clear day. The spray from this phenomenon can be carried a great distance, leading people to believe that it has started to rain. This sight can only be seen when the wind is in the right direction, when it becomes trapped in the cleft so the only way out is up, when it takes the waterfall with it. It is a most unusual sight and has to be seen to be believed.

The second phenomenon is to see the Kinder Downfall iced over. Many people make the long hard trek to view and photograph this winter spectacle. It is a popular place for climbers to practice ice techniques. Most people whether it be summer or winter, who are within the vicinity nearly always make for the Downfall as a resting place. Whilst having refreshment they can take in the panoramic view of the valley below.

KINDER EDGE GR.085898
Formerly The Black Edge in 1627, however, today it is also known as Black Ashop Edge, but generally referred to as the Edge. The actual Edge is about 2 miles (3kms.) long and lies on the north-western escarpment of Kinder. The highest point along the Edge is 2049ft. (624m) high. Along the Edge there are many places where it is extremely dangerous for the drop can be quite sheer, so be wary. The Edge is best walked along on a bright clear day for there are many sights to see along the Edge itself. Amongst them are fragments of two crashed Sabres, the Boxing Glove stones and many kinds of rock formations. There are also plenty of rock climbing areas to be found along here. Looking outwards from the Edge at various points you can see the following:- Snake Pass Summit and road, Black Ashop Moor, Ashop Clough, Featherbed Top and Moss, Bleaklow, The Snake Plantation, Hope Woodlands and on a very clear day the two B.B.C. Holme Moss Transmitters on the Yorkshire border.

KINDER HEAD (1829) GR.060880
Formerly called *Led Heyfelclyf* in the 12th century. It also goes by the name of the Cliff. Both names seem to conjure up a scene of a lofty rocky escarpment, when nothing could be further from the truth. It is in actual fact a gentle slope in the no access land on the banks of the Kinder Reservoir.

KINDER GATES GR.088887
The gates refer to two large prominent rocks on the Plateau through which the River Kinder flows. The Pennine Way lies between them and it is these two rocks which most are glad to see after wandering across the peaty Plateau for the best part of an hour. From this point the Kinder Downfall is only about three quarters of a mile away (1km.) along the River Kinder.

KINDER, JOHIS - KINDER, JOHN (see Kinders of Kinder)

KINDER LOW (1840) GR.079871
For some reason this area always fascinates me, though why I just do not know for the terrain here is barren. At a height of 2077ft. (633m) there stands an O.S. pillar and all around you is desolation. There is very little here in the way of scenery and yet it holds that certain

something. The terrain is a mixture of jet black peat, not mushy and squelchy, but rather soft and at the same time firm underfoot. Inter mingled with this are a number of large boulders of varying sizes. A few paces south-west of the pillar is a large stone cairn; the probable site of a burial chamber of long ago. From this area you can take in a bird's eye view of the Kinder Plateau, the desert of peat.

KINDERLOW CAIRN AND TUMULUS GR.073867

The south-west spur of Kinder is the location of this ancient burial mound now capped by a cairn of stones and rocks. To climb the spur from either Harry Moor or Broad Clough can be quite trying as there is no direct path up to the summit. One side of the spur is mainly a mixture of grass and a few small rocks whilst the opposite side is extremely rocky and boulder strewn. I find the best route and easiest is via the Swine's Back and Edale Rocks. Once the summit is attained you will find a very good vantage point here to view the valleys below whilst behind lies the Kinder Plateau.

KINDERLOW END (1840) GR.068866

This is the same spur which is capped by the tumulus and cairn of the above text, it is on the spur that the infamous Kinder Cavern is to be located. If attempting the direct climb up the spur be very careful especially in winter for it can be extremely slippery clambering over the rocks. Descending presents the same problem, so be wary.

KINDER PARISHES

To fully appreciate the extent of Kinder Scout you have to look at the parish boundary lines. There are nine in all. Admittedly one or two of the parishes only take in one or two points of Kinder, but it does not detract from the fact that these points fall within that parish. The nine Civil Parishes listed here are in no particular order.

C.P. Aston (1285)
: Formerly Estone in 1086. Embraces Win Hill and surrounding area.

C.P. Thornhill
: Formerly Thornhulle (1200), Tornhull (1230), Thornhill (1285) and Thornell in 1450. A variation of 'thorn bush hill'. This parish takes in the Yorkshire Bridge area.

C.P. Hope Woodlands
: Formerly Woodland (1577) and Woodland Hamblett (1689). The main points this parish takes in are Ashop

Clough, Ashop Head, Ashop Moor, Blackden Barn, Blackley Clough/Hey, Dean Hill, Dry Clough, Dunge Clough, The Edge, Fairbrook Naze, Featherbed Top, Glead Hill, Ladyclough, Seal Flats/Edge, Snake Inn, Thomasons Hollow, Urchin Clough, Woodlands Valley and last but not least Wooler Knoll.

C.P. Edale

Embraces a large slice of the southern section of Kinder.

C.P. Hayfield

Embraces another large slice, this on the western section of Kinder.

C.P. Hope

Formerly Hope (926), Peniarth (1086), Hoppa (1169), Hoppe (1188) and Hawpe in (1541). This parish takes in six main points which are: Bagshaw Bridge, Crookstone Barn/Hill/Knoll, Hope Brink and the Madwoman's Stones.

C.P. Chapel en le Frith

Former names are numerous. This parish takes in Colborne and Toot Hill. Whilst Roych Clough/Tor is shared with Chinley, Buxworth and Brownside Civil Parish.

C.P. Chinley, Buxworth and Brownside

Former names are Chinley:- Maystonfield (1610). Buxworth:- Buggesworthe (1275), Boggesworthe (1285), and Bugsworth until quite recently.

Brownside:- Bronsydy (1519) and Brownesyde (1585). The main points of the parish are Brown Knoll and South Head whilst the extreme south-west is shared with Chapel en le Frith.

C.P.Charlesworth (1767)

Formerly Cheuenwrde (1086), Chasseworth (1285) and Chalseworth (1577). This parish embraces all the moorland below the north-west escarpment of Kinder Scout.

KINDER PLATEAU GR.095887 (approx. centre)

The Plateau takes in about twenty square miles of god forsaken desert criss-crossed by peat groughs, some as deep as fifteen feet (5m). The average rainfall is 63 inches (160cms.). This can make the crossing very leg weary. After a downpour, the Plateau becomes a battlefield and you are the enemy.

Trying to cross the Plateau in a straight line is almost an impossibility, because you are forever dropping down into the groughs then scrambling out of them or trying to go round them. Dropping into them on the assumption that you would rather trace them in your general direction of travel is foolhardy, for they twist and turn, zig-zag this way and that way and are forever switching back upon themselves. This can add a good mile or so to your journey. Attempting the up-and-down, in-and-out way over these groughs for a long distance will make your legs very weary; they will feel like lumps of lead, especially after rain. It is very foolish to cross the Plateau without a compass, for besides wandering off-course - which is a dead cert, you have the added danger of the Peak mists which can and often do suddenly appear from nowhere. These mists are bad enough when you are on firm ground, let alone on sodden peat and the hidden grough pools which are often very deep with water. The best time to cross the Plateau is after a very hard frost for then the ground becomes rock hard, and where it takes an hour normally to cross a section it will only take about half that time after a frost. In all fairness, the Plateau does hold hidden dangers and is only recommended for the experienced walker, but it is nowhere near as bad as crossing the dreaded Bleaklow.

KINDER PRINTWORKS GR.048868 (site only)
Do not go looking for this 19th century calico works, for it has long since been demolished. It was built in the 1860's on what is now the Hayfield campsite. The printworks did not survive for too long, 50 years at the most and in all its existence there was nothing but trouble and strife, its tall chimney was felled in 1908.

KINDER RESERVOIR GR.057882
This picturesque reservoir is at its finest on a sunny day, and best viewed from high vantage points. The reservoir was built at the turn of the century for the Corporation of Stockport. There was a single track railway line linking the workings with Hayfield through the Kinder Bank Valley. Along the valley were many huts and buildings of various descriptions for the workers and their families.

The reservoir submerged the site of a medieval smelting works, a bridle path and a holding called Lower House. On the embankment called Kinder Head stood a house of the same name, this also had to be demolished to make way for the water catchment.

KINDER RESERVOIR MOUNTAIN RESCUE KIT GR.054882
The kit is available for mountain rescue in extreme emergency. It is located below the reservoir's dam in the pump and sluice house.

KINDER SCOUT (1767) GR.087876
Formerly Chendre (1086), Kender (1280), Kynder (1294), Kunder (1299), Kyndre (1315) and Chynder in 1554. It seems that nobody was sure what to call or pronounce the highest point in the Peak District, but they seemed to have sorted it out by 1767. Kinder Scout is the given name to the actual summit, the Plateau. The moors and surrounding countryside come under the jurisdiction of the local villages, townships and hamlets. People though tend to refer to Kinder as the whole massif from Hayfield to Yorkshire Bridge, Glossop to Edale and Ladybower to Brownside. (see also Chendre)

KINDER SCUT (see Kinder Downfall)

KINDERS OF KINDER GR.052874
The name 'Kinder' crops up frequently in the early records of the Parish of Hayfield; one of the earliest references dates back to 1640. Documents seem to indicate that they held a small freehold in the Kinder Valley, Hayfield. It may well have been The Cote, a smallholding halfway between Booth and Bowden Bridge. Certainly in the year 1820 a certain John Kinder owned The Cote. After this period the Kinder name becomes rather sketchy, then disappears altogether.

A curious fact emerges from all this, in that any reference to the Kinders of Kinder from the 17th to the 19th century always refer to the same christian name of John or Johis (meaning John) Kinder.

KINDER SUMMIT GR.087876
The summit is located in the middle of nowhere, namely the desert of the Kinder Plateau. The actual summit seems debatable because it does appear that one or two of the knolls around the summit do seem higher. However, rest assured that this area is the highest point of Kinder, in fact it is the highest point of the whole Peak District. The height is 2088ft. (638m).

There is no direct path of any description to the old pile of stones and stake that marks the summit, so your best bet is to take a compass bearing. The ideal places to take a bearing from are Pym Chair, Crowden Tower, Edale Rocks and Kinderlow O.S. pillar. I must stress that attempting to find the location in bad weather could lead to all kinds of trouble.

KINDER TRESPASS

Sunday April 24th 1932 will forever go down in the history of Kinder Scout, for on this day 400 ramblers assembled at the Bowden Bridge Quarry in protest at the landowners' and gamekeepers' refusal of rights-of-way over Kinder. After the rally the ramblers then marched up Williams Clough, where they were joined by a contingent of ramblers from over the border, Sheffield. It was planned to trespass upon the summit of the Scout but the way was barred by a small party of gamekeepers. Minor skirmishes broke out but nothing serious. Finding the way barred, the ramblers re-routed themselves onto Middle Moor where they held a 'victory meeting'. After this meeting the ramblers then split up and made their own way to their respective destinations. A large contingent made their way back to Hayfield Station where they were met by the police, who arrested six people whom they designated and identified as the ringleaders. A few weeks later at the Derby assizes five of the accused namely:- Anderson, Clyne, Nassbaum, Rothman and Gillett were sentenced to prison terms of between two and six months. However the ball had started rolling, slowly mind you, but it gathered momentum as the years passed by till finally rights-of-way were established.

KINDER VALLEY GR.037869 - 053880

This valley is approximately two miles (3kms.) long and entertains the River Sett for one half and the River Kinder for the other. The valley starts at Hayfield town centre and follows the course of these connecting rivers through to the Kinder Reservoir.

When the construction of the reservoir was in progress at the turn of the century, a railway linked Hayfield with the reservoir through this valley. (see Kinder Valley Train)

The valley has seen quite a number of changes in the last hundred years of which many are to be found in this book. (see Nanny Goat Junction, Kinder Printworks, Kinder Village, Hayfield Campsite and Kinder Reservoir)

KINDER VALLEY MISSION GR.051873

The mission was built for the workers and their families who were working on the construction of the Kinder Reservoir at the turn of the century. The mission was well attended every Sunday for worship. Upon the completion of the reservoir only a handful of people remained, so to offset this, it was decided to open the mission for a period of between four to five weeks in the summer to take in children on school holidays. This lasted a number of years until even this scheme died a death. The mission fell into decay and is now just a pile of rubble in the undergrowth.

KINDER VALLEY TRAIN

This train ran along the Kinder Waterworks Railway through the Kinder Valley. The train hauled materials from Hayfield Station through to the Kinder Reservoir when it was under construction. En route the train would stop at various pick-up points to let the workers on and off. Though the railway was only a short one it managed to take in a couple of bridges, sweeping curves and even a wooden trestle bridge.

Very little evidence remains today of the railway, in fact it seems impossible that a train ever steamed through the valley, for there is no visible evidence of there ever being a railway track.

KINDER VILLAGE GR.053871

This village occupied the land between Bowden Bridge and the construction of the Kinder Reservoir at the turn of the century. Today, anyone passing by here on a sunny day admiring the sheep and their offspring, would be hard pressed to believe that here once stood a ramshackle town of huts, shacks, tents and other forms of abode, lining these pleasant meadows.

The village was often referred to as 'Tin Town', as were most of these hastily erected villages for construction workers at the latter end of the last century and the beginning of this century. The term arose from the structure of these buildings for the basic material used was tinplate. The particular workers here were employed by the Corporation of Stockport for the building of Kinder Reservoir. Generally speaking they were a happy lot and many were sad that they had to leave the area upon the completion of the reservoir. One or two even managed to settle in the area and eke out a living.

KINDER WATERWORKS RAILWAY (see Kinder Valley Train)
KINDERWODEBROC (see River Kinder)
KINGS LAND (see Chendre)
KENDER (see Kinder Scout)

KIRKSTEADS GR.050871

Though it is not recorded on any O.S. map it is regarded and widely assumed that Kirksteads was where Bowden bridge and the cottage now stand. Another belief is that since man arrived in the area long ago a dwelling of some form has been in existence at this spot, for man tended to build where two rivers joined forces. This is also the place where Heathfield Chapel was erected in the 11th century, so we are led to believe. Alas, no sign of the chapel can be found, moreover Kirksteads has also disappeared.

KNOTT MR. & MRS. (see Farlands)
KUNDER AND KYNDER (see Kinder Scout)
KYNDER BANKE (see Kinder Bank)
KYNDRE (see Kinder Scout)

—L—

LADY BOOTH GR.142866
This non existent booth is more often than not confused with Nether Booth, as a lot of the land and buildings around Nether Booth began with the prefix 'Lady'! In fact there is in Nether Booth a riding school called by the name Ladybooth Riding School. About two hundred years ago a very small hamlet stood on the banks of the Lady Brook, not far from where the Rowland Cote Youth Hostel now stands and this in all probability was the hamlet of Lady Booth. It was only a small cluster of buildings which after a period of time became vacant and were never inhabited again, resulting in the buildings deteriorating. The stone from the buildings was used by the local farmers for their own purposes, till eventually all trace of Lady Booth disappeared.

LADY BOOTH BROOK (1706) GR.141865
A meandering brook that cuts a ravine stretching from Rowland Cote Moor down to Nether Booth. The terrain the brook flows through is a mixture of marsh, trees, shrubs and small rocks. The commencement of its journey begins near the Druids Stone where a number of small tributaries flow together on a sodden stretch of Rowland Cote Moor. It then falls down, cascading at various places till it meets up and is swallowed by the River Noe. Midway along the brook and overlooking it is the splendid youth hostel called Rowland Cote.

LADYBOOTH HALL AND FARM (see Nether Booth)
LADYBOOTH RIDING SCHOOL (see Nether Booth)

LADY CLOUGH GR.096928
Formerly the Ladie Brook and Clough End in 1627. Another of my favourite cloughs, this being the first clough past the Snake Pass

Summit in the direction of the Snake Inn. It lies in the shadows of the Snake Road and the Salvin Ridge. A meandering brook flows the length of the clough eventually meeting up with the River Ashop. The feeders of the brook mainly flow off the Hope Woodlands of Bleaklow, passing under the Snake Road. Some of these feeders are quite impressive, cascading out from miniature waterfalls to feed the brook.

LADY CLOUGH FOREST GR.107917

Basically a continuation of the above clough, though in complete contrast. The area here is surrounded by the tall conifers of the Ladyclough Forest and Snake Plantations. There are numerous lay-bys for cars along this stretch of the Snake Road, usually at access points. There is a trail through the forest and it goes by the name of the Lady Clough Forest Trail.

LADY CLOUGH MOOR GR.100921

A moor of contrasts, for the land is divided into three segments. The top of the moor is heavily gouged out with those boot-clogging peat groughs whilst the middle flanks are thick in moss and bracken. The lower regions encase the moor with the scenic conifers of the Lady Clough Forest.

LADY OF THE STAIRS GR.052865

The lady in question refers to a wandering spirit that walked the stairs of Stones House, Heyfield. Legend tells of a black-clad woman, old in appearance, who supposedly walked up the stairs of the old house. A number of people claim to have seen a ghost-like figure pass by a window on its way up the stairs. This story dates back a few years, but since the house has been renovated no more sightings have occurred

LANDS BARN (see Oller Brook)

LEE ESTATE, FARMHOUSE AND COTTAGE GR.097856

A quite large estate which stretches in length from Upper Booth to the packhorse bridge at the foot of Jacob's Ladder. This land does not fall within the boundary of open access but it does fall within the bounds of the National Trust. The main path through this estate follows the course of the Pennine Way alternative route through to Jacob's Ladder, or in the opposite direction to Upper Booth. Beside this path there are one or two minor paths, mainly on the Tagnaze side for Rushup Edge. The farmhouse-cum-cottage lies midway along the main route through the estate, the buildings being as one are typical of the early 18th century stone farmhouses. A hundred years ago this row of buildings was commonly known as 'The Lee'.

LEYGATEHEAD MOOR (1840) GR.055895
Formerly the name was split into two words being, Leygate Head Moor. What can I say about this moor, for it is very tiresome and unattractive as well as being a desolate place. Most ramblers are glad to reach the end of this tract of land and who can blame them! I strongly advise you to carry a compass on this moor, for if you stray off the one main path in a mist the chances are that you will become totally disorientated.

LIBERATOR (see Kinder Aircraft Crash Sites)
LITELHAYFELD (see Little Hayfield)

LITTLE HAYFIELD GR.034882
Formerly Parva Heyfeld (1250), Parva Hayfeld (1285) and Litelhayfeld (1427). It may be little in stature but it has a large reputation for the pleasant and fairly easy walks around the surrounding countryside, for people of all ages. It is a small hamlet lying off the A624 opposite Park Hall entrance. The hamlet is encased in the pleasant surrounds of small woods and you will find Little Hayfield very picturesque if you view it from the hills overlooking it in the summer when all plant life is in full bloom. Alternatively from the same viewpoint in winter on a sunny day, you will find it most charming when it is blanketed with fresh crisp snow.

LOWER BOOTH (see Nether Booth)

LOWER HOUSE GR.056882 submerged.
This was a fine old building that stood in direct line with Upper House, but whereas Upper House stands upon the higher regions overlooking the Kinder Reservoir, Lower House stood down in the valley below. This was its downfall, for now it lies within the area of the Kinder Reservoir Dam, submerged under all that water, lost forever to mankind.

—M—

MADWOMAN'S STONES (1840) GR.138881
Situated on the north-eastern side of Upper Moor, this jumble of flat

topped rocks marks the boundary line of the parishes of Edale and Hope. From the stones you can take in some excellent views of the opposite moors, namely the Hope Woodlands and the towering Alport Castles. How did these stones come by their curious name? Perhaps some woman in an era long gone committed a dastardly deed here!

MAREPIECE WOOD GR.051878

A wood that stands on the banks of the Kinder Road, Hayfield, facing the holdings of Farlands and Booth. There is quite an abundance of trees which meet up with the part-dead Oldpits Plantation. At its northern end lies an old quarry where the proud Heron Rock can be seen overlooking the wood. Though it is generally thought that this wood is a no-go area to the public, access is possible via the main entrance onto White Brow by the side of the Kinder Reservoir, then doubling back along a small path which passes through the quarry into the wood. The path meanders through the wood and exits out onto the Oldpits Plantation.

MARRIOT, SAMUEL AND MARRIOT'S PLACE
(see Hill's House, Hayfield)
MARSHALL, JACOB (see Edale Head House and Jacob's Ladder)
MAYSTONFIELD (see Kinder Parishes)

MERMAID'S POOL (1840) GR.075887

Lying on a small plateau above the Peter Nook Wood, this quite large and deep pool has an ancient legend attached to it. The legend says that if you want everlasting life, then you should make the journey to the pool every Easter Sunday in the early hours of the morning. Upon reaching the pool you must sit down on the banking. If by chance a mermaid pops her pretty little head up and then emerges from the pool you will receive your wish of everlasting life. One Hayfield gentleman, at the turn of the century, used to make the pilgrimage every year, but he must have missed the last one. He died aged 103!

MICAH'S CHURCH (see Four Jack's Cabin)

MIDDLE MOOR GR.045885

Formerly More (1346), Heyfield Moor (1640) and Hayfield Moor in 1830. Much the same terrain as Leygatehead Moor; Middle Moor connects to Leygatehead, so the least said about the terrain the better. Two main paths cross this black moor, one from Carr Meadow the other being the Snake Path from Hayfield. Both of these paths join up at a white shooting cabin. Near this cabin is a dangerous bog, normally it will not bother you unless you are attempting the climb up the Knot, or you are coming or going from Carr Meadow. Heed all notices and cross by the wooden footbridge provided or else you will be in trouble.

MIDDLE SEAL CLOUGH (see Seal Flats)
MILES HAWK (see Kinder Aircraft Crash Sites)

MILL HILL GR.062904

Formerly The Milne Hill in 1640. No mill here but there is a hill, the name 'Mill' may stem from the medieval times when there used to be a smelting works in the vicinity. At a height of 1761ft. (537m), it can be said that Mill Hill stands at the crossroads of the north-western region of Kinder. This is shown by a guide post found at the base of the hill and at the top of Williams Clough. From this guide post you have a choice of five main routes. Firstly over Leygatehead Moor and Burnt Hill to the Grouse Inn, secondly down through Williams Clough to the Kinder Reservoir or onto Middle Moor via the Snake Path. Thirdly up the western buttress of the Kinder Edge, fourthly along the Pennine Way over the Featherbed Moss to Bleaklow and finally along the Snake Path through Ashop Clough to the Snake Inn.

The wreckage of a liberator bomber can be viewed about a five minute walk from the summit of Mill Hill.

MILL HILL ROCKS GR.067897

These rocks are not on Mill Hill, in fact they face the hill, being a rocky crag on the north-western buttress of Kinder overlooking Williams Clough. An excellent place for the inexperienced rock climber, for it abounds in routes.

MILLSTONES AND OLD SMITHY GR.077877

The site of this once prosperous smithy can be located within the jumble of rocks known as Cluther Rocks. About two hundred years ago this area rang with the sound of mallet and chisel in the making of millstones, which were then transported down the hillside to the various mills in the locality. There is still the odd millstone to be found here and there on the hillside; remarkably, some are still in very good condition.

MISTY BUTTRESS GR.096896

Located on the eastern edges of the Fairbrook Naze, this buttress, a favourite with the novice rock climbers, earns its name through the low clouds that always seem to hang around here. Apart from the rock climbing aspect, there are some splendid views from here, especially over the Woodlands Valley.

MORE (see Middle Moor and Upper Moor, Hayfield)
MOSS CASTLE (see Glead Hill)

MOUNTAIN RESCUE POSTS AND KITS
CROWDEN Y.H. - GR.074994
FIELDHEAD, EDALE - GR.124856
GLOSSOP - GR.036943
KINDER RESERVOIR (kit only) - GR.054882

There are quite a number of rescue posts in the Peak District, three of which are located in the Kinder area and another not far off at Crowden, serving mainly the Black Hill and Bleaklow areas.

We should be grateful for these volunteers who risk injury to themselves when called out in all kinds of weather. All credit to them and long may they thrive. Donations are much appreciated for the upkeep of their equipment etc. Most information centres have a donation box.

MOUNTAIN VIEW GR.052874

Mountain View referred to a bungalow that was erected for the workers on the construction of the Kinder Reservoir, and it remained standing for some fifty years. Not long after the completion of the reservoir the bungalow became empty, the tenancy was taken over by a married couple with the surname Bashford. They set about converting the bungalow into a cosy little café, the Mountain View, which became the first café after leaving Kinder or the last before attempting Kinder on the Hayfield side. Either way the Bashford's were on to a winner, for this was during the boom years of the rambling scene in the 30's and 40's.

The demise of the café came when Mr. Bashford died and his wife decided to move. This left the way clear for Mr. J.Watts, who owned the land, to have the bungalow pulled down.

Passers by can still see the foundations of Mountain View.

MOUNT FAMINE (1829) GR.056852

Not quite a mountain but from certain angles it does resemble one, more so in winter when it is capped by snow. Once the summit has been attained there are some splendid views to enthral you.

Immediately below is the South Head Farm and the surrounding valley, whilst above rises Kinder itself. Turning to face south-west you can take in the long Cracken Edge where a bit further along it meets up with the Ollersett Moor. On its western flank there runs the old roman road of Highgate, on the opposite eastern flank there is the Dimpus Gate Track, and towering above is the majestic South Head Hill.

The name seems to stem from a folklore tale, which implied that cattle used to feed here, but by some quirk of nature they never fattened up, hence the name of the hill.

Another curious tale, though this time true, is that about 150 years ago there used to be a bakery situated at the base of Mount Famine, overlooking Southhead Farm. It was well away from the busy village of Hayfield, but the baker was not as daft as he might appear. He chose this spot because it was a central position for all the bridle paths leading to villages and farms at Chapel en le Frith, Chinley, Edale, Kinder and Hayfield.

MUSHROOM GARDEN (see Woolpacks)

—N—

NAB BROW (1830) GR.058885

The brow stands on the northern banks of Kinder Reservoir, at the foot of Williams Clough. If you stand on the bend of the brow, you will have a splendid view of the western edges of Kinder, also at this bend is the junction of the two main paths from Hayfield. Firstly the path from next to the entrance of the reservoir that leads up to Nab Brow via White Brow, secondly the Snake Path from Hayfield that drops down off Middle Moor just above the meeting of the two paths.

NAGS HEAD INN GR.124860

Now called 'The Old Nags Head Inn', this old stone and timbered inn was built in 1620, and is generally termed the starting place of the Pennine Way. This inn was the first official Peak District Information Centre. (see Heardman, Fred)

On a summer's day the inn looks quite serene and picturesque, whilst on a winter's night it is likened to a Christmas card.

NANNY GOAT JUNCTION GR.051872

The location of this very small station was to be found near Bowden Bridge and Oak Bank Cottage. The station was used by the workers on the construction of Kinder Reservoir at the turn of the century. Upon the completion of the reservoir the railway and station were dismantled, and nothing is left to remind us of it. Oak Bank House is the approximate location of the site of Nanny Goat Junction.

NETHER BOOTH (1625) GR.142861
This booth has had a number of aliases over the centuries which have included Lower Booth and Lady Booth. Nether Booth is a very small hamlet through which runs the main road. As it is basically a farming community drivers should beware. The booth was built up around the Old Nether Booth Farm which has changed very little over the years. Other buildings which make up the booth include Ladybooth Hall and farm also the Ladybooth Riding School - this is why Nether Booth is often mistaken for the long lost Lady Booth. As you approach the booth from the west there is a side gate and entrance that will take you up to the Rowland Cote Youth Hostel.

NETHER GATE CLOUGH GR.098910
A steep flanked clough that is part rocky and can be very marshy in certain places. Through it flows a feeder for the River Ashop. The clough starts its small illustrious journey off the Lady Clough Moor and Salvin Ridge, which both provide tributaries for the clough feeder.

NETHER MOOR GR.147875
Formerly Nethermore in 1659. Very fern laden on its steep sided flanks in the summertime, but the flat top of this moor is something else, a feet-tripping and hole-ridden area covered in bracken that hides the ground, so be wary. The moor lies below the plateau of the Upper Moor and at the summit of Jagger's Clough. The land is featureless and the only item of interest here lies at its western end where there is to be found the remains of an ancient burial chamber, which is also the site of a Druid's altar.

NETHERMORE (see Nether Moor)
NETHER OLLERBROOK (see Ollerbrook Booth)

NETHER RED BROOK (1840) GR.086898
A brook that runs parallel with the Upper Red Brook, both of which flow off the Kinder Edge and down through the Black Ashop Moor, eventually ending up feeding the River Ashop. The summit of the Nether Red Brook is extremely rocky but you will be very disap-

pointed if you expect to find the brook cascading over the edge onto these rocks, for at this point it is only a trickle; filling up more as it gathers the small feeders off Black Ashop Moor.

NETHER TOR (1840) GR.124876
A large amphitheatre of sheer rocks that stand proudly overlooking the scenic Grindsbrook Clough. This tor along with its sister, Upper Tor, found a short distance away, is probably the most used playground for rock climbing in the Kinder area. These tors are only advisable for the experienced climber, as extreme care must now be observed because the rock face is badly eroded.

NETHER SEAL CLOUGH (see Seal Flats)

NOE STOOL GR.084869
Formerly Nowstoolehill (1577) and Nowstool Hill (1610). If you are looking for no stool in particular then will you find Noe Stool? This is an extremely large boulder perched overlooking Edale Head. It is another one of Kinder's famous landmarks and can be seen quite clearly from a number of positions. Another name it is often called by is the 'Anvil'; its shape tells you why. It is an awkward rock to scramble up, though on one side someone has taken the trouble to carve out some notches, desecrating the noble rock. The origin of its name stems from the River Noe, which starts is maiden journey from below the rock amongst the cloughs below.

NOUE AND NOWE (see River Noe)
NOWSTOOLEHILL AND NOWSTOOL HILL (see Noe Stool)

NUNGRAIN BRINK (1840) GR.112904
A steep incline which rises from the Woodlands Valley opposite the Snake Inn to below the Fairbrook Naze. It is not a very good area or terrain to walk over, though there is a path but it is not well defined. The name is derived from the nuns of St. Mary's, Derby, who owned land hereabouts in the 12th century.

NUNGRAIN DITCH/DYKE GR.108903
A fissure which is almost a perfectly straight line, splitting the upper regions of Nungrain Brink. It is a natural fissure some eight to ten feet wide in places, whilst the depth can reach about seven feet. The length of the fissure is quite unusual for a natural straight line. It starts at the summit of Urchin Clough then passes over the Brink, eventually

tapering off into the Fair Brook opposite the Nether Seal Clough.

—O—

OAK BANK COTTAGE GR.050871
A very versatile cottage, for in its lifespan it has been a cosy cottage, a foreman's lodge, a small grocer's-cum-ironmonger's shop, an abode for farmers who had served their time out upon the land, dog kennels and now once again a renovated country cottage.

The cottage sits close to the Bowden Bridge Cottage on the Kinder Road, Hayfield and though it has changed dramatically over the years from the original wooden and stone structure of its heyday to the stone cottage of today, it still holds an aura of charm.

OAKEN CLOUGH (1840) GR.068858
A half and half clough with only the higher regions of the clough falling within the boundary of open access, yet the whole of the clough falls within the boundary of the National Trust. The clough starts at the Stonyford Crossing and then falls sharply to finish up close to the Southhead Farm. The brook which flows down the clough starts its journey up on Kinder Low and finally ends up marrying the River Sett.

OLD NAG'S HEAD INN (see Nag's Head Inn)

OLDPITS PLANTATION GR.048878
An area situated above Kinder Bank and Marepiece Wood where there was at one time a flourishing plantation of trees that grew on a large flat plateau. Sadly the plateau is now only a graveyard for most of the trees; trunks and stumps of the dead trees rise out of the ground like headstones and crosses. This is how the Kinder Plateau would have looked a thousand years or more ago. It is an eerie place when visited in a thunderstorm, also at dusk and at the dead of night. It is certainly worth a visit at night providing you are not of a nervous disposition.

Access is gained mainly via the Snake Path and Heron Rock, though there is a small path through Marepiece Wood.

OKEN NABBE (see The Nab)
OLERBROCKE, OLLERBROKE AND OLLERBROKE BOOTH (see Ollersbrook Booth)

OLLER BROOK AND OLLERSBROOK CLOUGH GR.128862 LAND'S BARN GR.127861

Oller Brook formerly Alder Brook, flows through the Ollerbrook Clough, both of which start near the summit of Blackden Edge, between Rowland Cote Moor and the Ringing Roger. The brook eventually flows through the hamlet of Ollerbrook Booth then carries on for a short distance before it is taken over by the River Noe. The long brook tumbles down through the clough over many rocks and is flanked on both sides by steep rising banks. The going underfoot becomes quite stony and rocky near to its summit where close by can be found the remains of a Wellington Bomber.

Land's Barn (formerly The Land in 1670) is what the name implies, 'a barn' and is situated within the base of the Ollerbrook Clough close to Ollerbrook Booth.

Only a very small portion of this area falls within the open access so please respect the land. Open access is fully reached at the summit of the clough.

OLLERBROOK BOOTH (1603) GR.128859/ NETHER OLLERBROOK GR.130859

Ollerbrook Booth formerly Olerbrock (1561), Ollerbroke (1562) and Ollerbroke Booth (1596), is a small hamlet that is very slowly expanding and is swallowing up the tiny hamlet of Nether Ollerbrook which lies on Ollerbrook Booth's eastern side. Both of the hamlets stand in the middle of pasture land, yet a row of terraced houses, one of which is a shop, and stand on the main thoroughfare through Edale close by Edale Mill, falls within the jurisdiction of Ollerbrook Booth.

OLLERBROOK CLOUGH (see Oller Brook)

ORDNANCE SURVEY PILLARS (Triangulation Stations) GR. VARIOUS

The O.S. pillars, or trig points, are found throughout the length and breadth of Britain. There are several in the Kinder area, generally on summits or vantage points. Backpackers find them most helpful in very or vantage points. Backpackers find them most helpful in very inclement weather conditions for pinpointing their exact position. The following are pillars that are standing defiantly against the elements in the Kinder region:- Blackden Edge GR.129878; Brown Knoll GR.084851; Harry Hut GR.045908; Kinder Plateau GR.078894; Kinder Low GR.079871 and Win Hill GR.187851.

At one period the area was littered with more of them, including the following:- Crookstone Knoll GR.145884; Broadlee Bank Tor GR.112859; Nether Moor GR.148874; Seal Stones GR.114888 and White Brow GR.056884.

OVER HORSE WAIE (1609) GR.050870 - 103854
The name has long since gone for it referred to the bridle road between Hayfield and Edale via The Ashes, Coldwell Clough, Stonyford, Edale Cross, Jacob's Ladder (before it was called Jacob's Ladder) and then onwards into Upper Booth, Edale. The road is commonly known as Edale Road now, though the terrain has changed little. In wintertime you can almost guarantee that the section between Coldwell Clough Farm and Jacob's Ladder will be impassable, for it is not uncommon to have snowdrifts here to a depth of about six or seven feet (2m). This route, especially from Hayfield to Edale and not vice versa, can be walked in a pleasant steady four hours by anybody who is reasonably fit and has suitable walking shoes on. To walk it from Edale you have the daunting climb up Jacob's Ladder then the drag up to Edale Cross.

OXFORD (see Kinder Aircraft Crash Sites)

—P—

PARK HALL GR.037885
Formerly Parkehall (1577). The hall entrance is located opposite Little Hayfield, off the A624. The hall is unusual because it is crescent shaped and over the centuries has housed many a fine nobleman as well as the odd character here and there. The grounds sadly are not as splendid as they were a hundred years ago, and in fact the hall itself was left derelict for a good number of years at the turn of this century, but it has now found a new lease of life.

PARKIN CLOUGH GR.196851
A very steep and back-breaking climb up this clough will bring you out at the foot of the Winhill Plantation, where from here it is just a short walk to the summit of Win Hill. The path through the clough is known as the Yorkshire Bridge Track, which years ago used to be a packhorse route from Hope and Edale into Yorkshire.

The clough is easily located, for if you cross the Yorkshire Bridge over the River Derwent facing west, just walk to your right a few paces, pass through a gate and the clough then lies directly to your left. The path through the clough passes beneath towering conifer trees, and though quite scenic in one respect the climb can be one hard slog, especially in bad weather. The hazards you face include mud, loose stones, erosion of the path and numerous tree roots. If Win Hill is your destination then it is worth every leg-weary step. An alternative route to Win Hill is via the Thornhill Carrs Footpath. (see text)

PARVA HAYFELD AND PARVA HEYFELD (see Little Hayfield)

PEEP O' DAY (Hill's House) GR.048850
The Peep O' Day is another name for Hill's House, found about a mile and a half (2km.) along the A624 from Hayfield on its way to Chinley. The Peep O' Day is so named because on the eastern wall of the house is an eye window set in a plinth, as the sun rises in the morning the eye catches the first rays of the sun. You will have to be up early in the summer to see this spectacle.

PENIARTH (see Kinder Parishes)

PENNINE WAY
The Pennine Way was first thought up in 1935, with the name of the Jubilee Trail, (it was George V's jubilee year). Tom Stephenson was the innovator, though there was no actual route proposed at the time. A group of people formed The Pennine Way Association and by 1939 a route had been proposed, with a length of 180 miles (285kms.). By 1951 this had been extended to cover most of the now known route. The full route was officially opened in 1965.

The Pennine Way takes in a number of places - starting at Edale, the official starting point, the route stretches over the backbone of England to finish at Kirk Yetholm, a distance of 270 miles (420kms.) To walk the Pennine Way takes a lot of planning and forethought, and for full enjoyment of the walk you will need between 15 to 21 days.

Kinder has two Pennine routes; one is the official route over Kinder's soggy plateau or an alternative route for when weather conditions are not favourable which takes you up Jacob's Ladder and round by the Swine's Back then up to Kinder Low. People often agree that once you have Kinder, Bleaklow and Black Hill out of the way, the rest of the walk presents no problems to the backpacker underfoot!

PETER NOOK/WOOD GR.070885
The name is given to a small wood and the surrounding area around

the banks of the River Kinder, just below the confluence with the Red Brook. Though not big the wood can give adequate protection from the rain and is a favourite picnic spot with families on sunny summer days. In fact the River Kinder here is quite nice for there are one or two miniature waterfalls which look tempting and refreshing, especially if you feel sticky and sweaty!

PYM CHAIR GR.088869
The Woolpacks is the location of Pym Chair and is easily recognisable. It stands alone at the end of the Pagoda, a last bastion before crossing the plateau. Apart from the obvious chair shape it stands out because of its feature of having the shape of two large horns. The chair is reputed to be named after non-conformist minister John Pym who was supposed to have held meetings here in the 17th century.

—R—

RAMSLEY MOOR AND CLOUGH (1840) GR.065933
The moor falls away from the Snake Road and is very steep sided, whilst the terrain is barren of anything worth mentioning. The clough really starts on the other side of the Snake Road, splitting the clough into two, forming the Cabin Clough on the other side of the Snake. Through the clough and falling into the valley below is a brook which I find most enjoyable to watch as it cascades over the last few rocks before it is swallowed up by the Hurst Brook.

RED BROOK GR.076893
The brook flows off the plateau down a very rocky chasm through the Cluther Rocks then on to join up in wedlock with the River Kinder at Peter Nook's Wood. Standing on the summit of the brook and looking down it the view is marvellous. It is best viewed in the spring when the brook is usually in full flow; in summer the brook tends to dry up completely.

RED CLOUGH GR.086807
A clough that starts its life on the Featherbed Moss where several tributaries meet up to form Red Clough. The brook-cum-clough is then channelled down to the River Ashop which is lying in wait for the brook to feed it. An excellent bird's eye view of the clough can be obtained from the rocky escarpment of Kinder Edge.

RE-VEGETATION SCHEME

There are a number of small enclosures on and around Kinder, inside of which experiments are to be carried out to see if moorland grasses, heather and bilberry can flourish once again on the moors of Kinder. Atmospheric pollution is a major cause of the sparseness of vegetation on Kinder, but other reasons include the general public who tramp the moors, fires and sheep grazing. Co-operation in this scheme is required by all the public, so please keep out of the enclosures. The scheme will be in operation for a number of years.

RIDGE WOOD (see Slack Barn)

RINGING ROGER GR.125873

Also known as the Echoing Rocks, this is a magnificent escarpment of rocks that start to rise up gently from the east then reach a pinnacle on its western side. There are one or two vantage points from which to take in these proud rocks. Firstly there is the view of the pinnacle which can be viewed most dramatically from the boundary of open access at the base of the Golden Clough, and the second view I like most is at the northern end of The Nab above the Golden Clough, where you can take in Ringing Roger in all its magnificence.

The escarpment itself produces some of the most scenic views, for you can see Grindsbrook Clough, the Vale of Edale and the Great Ridge.

RIVER ASHOP (1627) GR.075907 - 165879

Formerly the Aqua de Essop (1215), Essope (1250) and Aqua de Eshop (1285). The river rises at Ashop Head in the shadows of the north west buttress of Kinder, and is formed by a number of minor feeders which is then in turn fed by a number of tributaries as it flows through the Ashop Clough. At this point it is fair to describe the river as only a narrow brook. After leaving the Ashop Clough it runs parallel with the Snake Road through the Woodlands Valley where it starts to widen out. The river ends its short but meandering journey when it flows into the head of the Ladybower Reservoir.

RIVER EDALE GR.084864 - 089861

Technically speaking this river does not exist, as it is the main western tributary of the River Noe. The River Edale is not even a mile long as the two tributaries that feed it and join together to form it beneath and in between Edale Rocks and the Noe Stool are actually longer than the river itself. Once the river has been formed, (it is only a fast flowing very narrow brook) it flows on down through the cloughs round

Jacob's Ladder to meet up at the old packhorse bridge merging together with other brooks to form the basis of the River Noe.

RIVER KINDER GR.089884 - 050870

Formerly Kinderwodebroc (1250) and Kinder Broocke (1640). The river rises on the Kinder Plateau between the two points of Kinder Low and Crowden Head. Exactly where it becomes a river is very debatable for there are close on a hundred minor feeders for the river on the plateau. One certain fact is that the river has taken its shape by the time it passes through the Kinder Gates, from where it arcs round to the Kinder Downfall tumbling over the edge to the waiting rocks below. From here it reverts back to a small brook passing by the Peter Nook Wood then on into the Kinder Reservoir. An outlet on the western side of the reservoir lets the river carry on its journey through the Kinder Valley. Journey's end comes at Bowden Bridge, where it meets up the with River Sett, the Sett taking over from this point onwards.

RIVER NOE (1636) GR.088862 - 205825

Formerly the Noue (1300) and Nowe (1330). The beginnings of this rather picturesque river are in the region of the old packhorse bridge at the base of Jacob's Ladder, where a number of tributaries here and a little bit further on help to swell it out a bit. The river flows through the Vale of Edale and the Hope Valley, and some of the finest views of the Peak can be seen from the banks of this river. Once through the booths of Edale it swings round and passes through Hope, onwards then through Brough until it is finally swallowed up by the magnificent River Derwent at Bamford.

RIVER SETT (1842) GR.073853 - 001853

The life of the River Sett starts out on the Dimpus Moor facing Edale Cross. Once the basic river has been formed it flows on, bypassing Southhead Farm, then onwards till it reaches Bowden Bridge where it meets up and digests the River Kinder. From here it flows on through the Kinder Valley until it reaches Hayfield, and once through Hayfield it gradually curves round to New Mills via Birch Vale and Thornsett. On attaining New Mills it passes through the towering gorge of The Torrs where the life of the Sett is terminated by the River Goyt.

ROUGH BANK AND URCHIN CLOUGH GR.105906

As the name implies, Rough Bank (formerly The Roughe Banck in

1627) is exactly this and it rises very sharply to 1650ft. (500m). The location of this bank is just inside the boundary of open access, opposite Saukin Ridge on the banks of the River Ashop. The bank is sandwiched between the Nungrain Brink and Urchin Clough.

Urchin Clough is one of those pleasant sort of cloughs, even though there is nothing special about it. The base, which starts at the River Ashop, is fairly rocky and the climb up by the cascading mini waterfalls is quite enjoyable. The clough's summit lies at the base of the Fairbrook Naze, a daunting climb.

ROUND STONES GR.089898
Exactly what they are, huge round-shaped stones located along the famed Kinder Edge between the Black Overhangs and the Suave Blocks.

ROWLAND COTE MOOR GR.134873
A rocky edge but not on the grandeur of Ringing Roger which is close by, though it does provide a very good vantage point to view the surrounding Peak District, especially from the Druid's Stone which stands along this edge. This rocky edge proves a defensive wall which stands on permanent guard over the rest of the moor below. This is very thick in moorland grass, resulting in a very tiresome walk up over the moor.

ROWLAND COTE YOUTH HOSTEL GR.149867
Once upon a time it used to be the residence of a member of the Batchelor family, famous for their peas and soups. Afterwards the house was completely renovated and can now accommodate over one hundred people. Access for vehicles is gained via Nether Booth then along a winding road to the scenic grounds of this splendid hostel.

ROWLEE BRIDGE GR.149891
It seems strange that a bridge of this large size should be here for once the opposite bank has been reached from the Snake Road there is nothing but moorland and a narrow track up to the smallholding at Upper Ashop. Part of the course of the ancient roman road between the forts of Melandra at Glossop and Navio at Brough link up with this double arched bridge which spans the River Ashop. There are quite a few farms on the Snake side but little else and no villages or towns for a good few miles.

ROYCH CLOUGH GR.080838
Formerly The Roch Clough (1620 and 1687). The Roache Clough (1640) and The Roiche Clough (1644). Roych Clough is in a no-access area, but the length of it means that at certain spots, footpaths and bridle paths can encroach upon or into it. The clough starts on the peat sodden Brown Knoll and then meanders down with the odd waterfall into the pleasant meadows of Brownside, coming out near to the entrance of the Cowburn tunnel, Chinley side. The clough is very steep sided in the upper regions, but the walk up it is fairly easy going until the Brown Knoll area is reached. The clough is well served by a number of tributaries coming down off the surrounding hills and moors, whilst the parish boundary of Chinley, Buxworth and Brownside follows the course of this meandering clough.

ROYCH TOR (1840) GR.083839
Formerly Catroche Torr (1601). A small rocky spur lying on the western fringes of Toot Hill and overlooking the large bowl in the middle of Roych Clough. Another place technically out of bounds to the backpacker for it lies smack in the middle of the no-access area. It can be accessible if you follow the minor footpaths and strictly adhere to them from the Roych Clough valley at its entrance near to the Cowburn tunnel opposite Malcoff Farm, Malcoff. The tor is nothing like the tors of the Grindsbrook Valley, Edale, but it does hold a certain aura. It is not advisable to seek out this tor after a very heavy snow storm, because it attracts snow like a magnet, completely encasing it in. This in turn creates a large overhang of snow which can fool a lot of people into believing that the edge of the rockface is where the snow ends. The danger also applies to walking below the tor; the snow can avalanche, and there's enough to suffocate you. You have been warned!

—S—

63 FIGHTER SQUADRON (see Kinder Aircraft Crash Sites)
627 SQUADRON (see Wellington Bomber, Blackden Edge. Kinder Aircraft Crash Sites)
SABRES (see Kinder Aircraft Crash Sites)
SALVIN RIDGE (see Featherbed Top)

SANDY HEYS (1840) GR.073893
Lying slightly westwards of the summit of the Kinder Downfall there is an area covering the edge of Kinder's Plateau that is rock strewn -

nothing towering, though there are some rocks that are slightly higher than the average person. Included within this rocky mass are the odd one or two little chasms which are very useful in bad weather or if you stop for refreshment and want to get out of the wind. On sunny days the rocks provide the backpacker with some splendid panoramic views of the valley below and the Cheshire landscape in the far distance.

SAUKIN RIDGE GR.110908

A slightly rocky area which is encased within the coniferous region of the Snake Plantation. The Snake Path starts/ends here and it is also the access point for Ashop Clough, boundary of open access. On a warm sunny day or in the evening as the sun is setting this is one of the best photographic beauty spots of the Kinder Massif. After walking the Snake Path from Hayfield, with the long trudge through the peat, mud and bogs of Ashop Clough the sight is heaven-sent and renews your sapping strength.

SEAL EDGE GR.105887

Formerly The Seele Edge (1627). On the north-eastern escarpment of Kinder lies the very rocky Seal Edge of which the Chinese Wall is the most prominent feature. I cannot explain why but this seems one of the most sought-after places on Kinder. Perhaps it is the views of the Woodlands Valley below, or across to the Hope Woodlands or the Snake Inn, nestling in a wooded clearing amongst the Snake Plantation. Then again it could be the rocky features of the edge itself where you have the picturesque ravine through which the Fair Brook flows whilst towering above the brook you have the craggy Fairbrook Naze. It may well be that it is sought-after due to a combination of all these features.

SEAL FLATS (1840), MIDDLE SEAL CLOUGH, NETHER SEAL CLOUGH AND UPPER SEAL CLOUGH GR.112894

Seal Flats, also known as Seal Moor, is not what the name seems to imply, being quite the opposite from flat! It is a wild barren moor which rises sharply from the banks of the River Ashop till it reaches the summit of the base of the rocky Seal Edge. A most inhospitable place of groughs and moorland heather, it also has three cloughs all of which flow into the Fair Brook, and one, Middle Seal Clough, has its brook actually flowing off Seal Edge. This particular clough is also the most rocky of the three.

SEAL MOOR (see Seal Flats)

SEAL STONES GR.116887
Much the same terrain as Seal Edge including the views. The stones lie on a spur which juts out between the Seal Flats and Blackden Moor.

SEVEN MINUTE CROSSING GR.121860
The quickest and shortest route across the Kinder Plateau, hence the name of this area. The points in question lie north to south between the summit of Blackden Edge near to the left of the Blackden Brook summit and then across to Dry Clough, right of Nether Tor. This may well be the narrowest point but care is still required in going in a straight line, especially in mist, for like the rest of the plateau the terrain abounds in peat groughs.

SHAW MOOR (1843) AND WORM STONES (1842) GR.044916
Another area of moorland heather, this moor is situated near the Glossop side of the Kinder Massif. Across the moor is a narrow footpath connecting the A624 near Charlestown, Glossop with Chunnal Moor and Harry Hut. The path passes over a crag with the curious name of the Worm Stones, which overlook the large Whitehorn Clough.

SHAW WOOD GR.118854
Formerly Shawood Field (1733). A small insignificant wood to the backpacker which lies at the foot of the Broadlee Bank Tor in a private field.

SHAWOOD FIELD (see Shaw Wood)
SHIRT, JOHN (see Edale Cross)

SHOOTING CABINS
Over the last two hundred years or so there have been numerous shooting cabins dotted about Kinder Scout. Most of these cabins have now completely gone with the reduction of game bird shooting on Kinder Scout. There are still one or two around Kinder which are used in the shooting season, these are mainly Middle Moor, GR.050883 and Whitehorn Clough out on Shaw Moor, GR.048913. Others are either in a very ruinous state or very little remains of them: Ashop Clough GR.091907; Dry Clough GR.119875 and 119871; Gateside Clough GR.117893; Span Clough GR.068925; Swine's Back

GR.076865 and Wove Hill GR.104879.

SKI RUN, GRINDSLOW KNOLL, EDALE

A lot of people find it hard to believe that there is a ski run for the public at Edale, but there is, and also a separate toboggan run. The ski run is situated just below the rocky crag of Grindslow Knoll overlooking Edale, where most weekends in the snow-laden months of winter, there can be found around two hundred skiers from all walks of life partaking in this winter sport. The ski run is only about half a mile in length, but it is adequate and there are plenty of other smaller slopes in the vicinity to practice on. Oddly enough, the patch of land was purchased for the run in 1959, the year of the big heatwave and drought!

SLACK BARN (1840) AND RIDGE WOOD GR.154869 - 158868

A barn that lies not far from Carr House whilst about the same distance behind the barn lies Ridge Wood. Though both places fall just in the boundary of the National Trust they both lie within farm grazing land and no paths or right-of-way are shown as yet.

SNAKE INN (1829) GR.113906

The inn which stands 1086 feet (331m) above sea level, was built in 1821 as a posting house for travellers between the Glossop and Sheffield turnpikes. The name derives from the coat-of-arms of the Cavendish family, who have the emblem of a snake. Until the 1920's there was a sign of the snake over the door of the inn. In both directions from the inn along the Snake Road are to be found small lay-bys for motorists, but there is no bus service along this route except on Sundays in summer when there is a very limited service.

SNAKE PATH GR.110907 - 041869

In the late 19th century the Peak District and Northern Counties Footpaths Preservation Society appealed for £1,000 to put forward their case that the Snake Path was an ancient right-of-way. Landowners tried their level best to thwart the Society, but after many lengthy discussions and negotiations they all came to an agreement, and the right-of-way was finally established in 1897.

The path stretches from the Snake Inn to Hayfield via the Ashop Valley, Williams Clough and Middle Moor; a distance of 6 miles (9kms.)

SNAKE PLANTATION GR.105915
This is a thickly wooded area of conifers, nearly 2 miles (3kms.) long, following the course of the Snake Pass Road. The general area is more widely known as the Lady Clough Forest, and the Forestry Commission has opened up a sizeable chunk for access. Many paths are to be found inside; please keep to these.

SOUTH HEAD GR.061845
Formerly Southhedd (1562). Viewed from afar this hill which stands at 1430ft. (494m) looks daunting to climb, but nothing could be further from the truth. Once the foot of the hill is reached the actual climb up is no more than ten minutes for even the slowest backpacker.

South Head lies on the far south-western tip of the boundary of open access and lies in direct opposition to Mount Famine, and viewed from certain angles they both resemble the humps of a camel. I would go as far as to say that South Head is a miniature Win Hill, capped by a small pile of stones. It commands a position where you can view the surrounding countryside in a complete 360° sweep, where every direction will hold your attention. Northwards the views take in Mount Famine, Gee Banks and the farms of the valley below, whilst farther on lies Kinder Bank and Heron Rock, both lying in the shadows of The Knot. North-eastwards lies the western escarpment of Kinder, Kinder Low and End, the Swine's Back and Edale Moor; below these we have the wild moorland of Dimpus and the Brown Knoll. Moving round you can take in Colborne, Toot Hill, Roych Tor, The Roych then round to Chinley and the land as far back as Buxton. Westwards you have Cracken Edge and Ollersett Moor, these places are just the tip of the iceberg. South Head is well worth a visit.

SOUTH HEAD FARM GR.061855
This farm is 1000ft. (304m) above sea level, making it one of the highest farms of the Kinder area. Set in a picturesque valley on the banks of the River Sett and lying in the shadow of Mount Famine, it is typical of all the local farms around here. The present farm which is now in the care of the National Trust, stands on the site of the original farm which was destroyed by fire in the 18th century. Across from the farm lies Dimpus Clough, where a dastardly deed was committed which also had connections with the original farm. See Dimpus Clough.

SOUTHHEDD (see South Head)

SPAN MOOR AND SPAN CLOUGH (1840) GR.065928
HURST MOOR GR.060925

Span Moor borders on the Glossop area and is a barren tract of wild moorland lying in the shadows of Hurst Moor, another barren tract of land. There are no paths of any description to help you cross these moors. Separating both is Span Clough which runs the length of the two moors. The only pleasant feature of all this terrain is the brook, flowing along through Span Clough and then into Hurst Reservoir, Glossop.

SPAR CLOUGH AND SPAW CLOUGH (see Hollin Head)
SPEAR, WING COMMANDER (see Mk xl Light Transport Anson, Kinder Aircraft Crash Sites)
SPRA HOUSE (see Spray House Wood)

SPRAY HOUSE WOOD/FARM GR.038892

Formerly Spray Howse (1650) and Spra House (1714). Another picturesque area when viewed from the old bridle path connecting Carr Meadow with the Kinder Reservoir. The farm lies off the Glossop - Hayfield Road (A624) not far from Little Hayfield, whilst the wood being only small in stature lies back from the farmhouse inside a hollow. Only the farmhouse roof can be observed from the old bridle path, but that does not mean the view is not worthwhile, for it is quite charming. For complete observation of the farm you must first attempt the knotty problem of stumbling and tripping up The Knot to reach the summit. Failing this, cross the A624 and take the side road to Blackshaw's Farm - halfway up this road turn around and you will see the farm very clearly.

SPRAY HOWSE (see Spray House Wood)

STEPHENSON, TOM

Innovator of the Pennine Way, for it was Tom who in 1935 wrote an article in a newspaper proposing a route along the Pennines, which he called at the time 'The Jubilee Trail', in commemoration of the Silver Jubilee of George V.

Consequently this led to the formation of the Pennine Way Association, who within four years had mapped out a proposed route using existing rights-of-way. However, it took a further twelve years before official approval was granted for local authorities to negotiate rights-of-way. 1956 dawned and part of the Pennine Way was officially opened by well-known dignitaries of the time and of course Mr.

Stephenson himself, secretary of the Ramblers' Association. Another nine years was to elapse before the complete Pennine Way was opened to the public.

STONES HOUSE (1829) GR.052865
A fine old fashioned stone farmhouse built in 1774 in the Peak style of the era. Oddly enough the present building stands on the site of an old wattle and daub affair, of which a little bit still remains, for it is known that a 'Stonehouse' was in existence some sixty to seventy years previous to the present building. The farm is situated in a secluded position overlooking the Hayfield campsite, where there is a better view now than a hundred years ago when the Kinder printworks dominated the view. Surrounding the house on two sides is the small Elle Bank Wood. Though the house is set in its own private grounds, a closer view may be obtained via the Elle Bank Wood, skirting the edges of the wood until you are adjacent with the house. At one period the house was reputed to be haunted. (see Lady of the stairs)

STONYFORD (1840) GR.073863
Plenty of stones in the brook here and hence the name, but you can stride across without actually using them. It lies on the old bridle path from Hayfield - Edale, known as Stonyford Crossing. Another path from Hayfield via Tunstead Farm and Harry Moor joins the main bridle path here. 1985 saw a programme set out in which the old dry stone walls around the crossing were rebuilt and a wooden stile erected for our convenience, giving access to either Harry Moor or Broad Clough.

SUAVE BLOCKS GR.092898
Pleasant is the right word for this terrain, which takes in the splendid views across the Ashop Valley. However, bland is a more apt word for the rock face here as it provides a very gentle climb over large blocks of rock.

SWINE'S BACK (1840) GR.078863
On the southwest slopes of Kinder, more or less in line with Edale Cross lies a hill, which viewed from certain angles resembles the back of a pig, and hence the name Swine's Back. I find the best view of the Swine's Back is out on the barren Dimpus, above the small ravine where the River Sett starts is meandering journey. Another fine view of it can be obtained from the Jacob's Ladder path where it overlooks The Cloughs.

The Pennine Way alternative route via Kinder Low to Kinder Downfall passes this way, skirting the actual hump, whilst the hill itself is fairly steep and around the summit can be found a couple of minor rocky escarpments. Once on top of the hill you will find a small flat plateau, and from around its perimeter you can take in some splendid views of the Edale Rocks, the Woolpacks, Kinder Low, Dimpus, Brown Knoll and Kinderlow End. I find that one of the best views of The Cloughs is to be found from up here.

Have a walk over the top of the Swine's Back, it may be the only time you get to walk on a pig's back!

—T—

TAGG, JOSEPH (see Yorkshire Bridge)

TAG'S NAZE GR.097848
Formerly Tag's Neys (1767). (see Horsehill Tor)

TERROR BRIDGE GR.053867
Strange goings-on at night give this bridge a bad name! The bridge spans the River Sett, at the junction of both access points to Hill's House, Tunstead Farm and the Ashes. About a hundred years ago a little girl out riding her horse was thrown and killed at this spot, and curiously enough almost a century later a similar accident happened - only this time the girl was more fortunate. Many a person crossing this bridge at night has complained of strange eerie feelings, though nobody has actually seen anything. This also includes yours truly!

THE ANVIL (see Noe Stool)
THE ARMCHAIR (see Upper Western Buttress)

THE ASHES (1767) GR.055864
A small wood overlooks the Ashes Farm which now belongs to the National Trust. The original farm was built in 1641 and rebuilt in the 19th century. The name is derived not from the small wood but from the charcoal pits of long ago in which the residue of iron slag, ashes and charcoal have been found. Until the turn of the present century the farm was reached by a fine drive of oak trees, but for some inexplicable reason the owner decided to have the trees felled. Where the trees were felled they remained, allowed to rot away. It was a shame really, for in the 1850's the trees around The Ashes were reputed to be the finest timber in the district.

THE BLACK EDGE (see The Edge)
THE CLIFFS (see Kinder Head)

THE CLOUGHS GR.087866
The Cloughs are to be found on the south-southwest slopes of Kinder, lying below the very rocky Woolpacks. This hillside is crossed with channels and small ravines, many with brooks meandering down into the valley below. These small brooks include the River Edale, and they form an impressive sight on a very sunny day, foaming and glinting in the sun. Once all the brooks have reached the valley (which passes beneath Jacob's Ladder) they form the basis of the River Noe, flowing onwards under the old packhorse bridge, Yongate. Lying on the hillside beneath the Woolpacks can be found fragments of two plane wreckages. If you are prepared to walk up The Cloughs then you are in for a hard slog, especially in inclement weather.

THE COTE (see Kinders of Kinder)
THE EDGE (see Kinder Edge)
THE FAIRE BROOK EDGE (see Fairbrook Naze)
THE FARRE BROOK (see Fair Brook)
THE INTACKE AND THE INTAKES (see Tom Heys)

THE KNOT (1843) GR.046894
A steep rising hill which stands proudly above and between Middle Moor and Hollingworth Clough. You either love it or hate it; I tend to lean to the former, especially in the snow laden winter months. The Knot is one of those places rarely visited by the backpacker, because it does not lie on any recognised route. Another reason is the heather and the moorland grass has so intermingled that it is quite a feat to reach the summit without tripping or stumbling, for there is no recognised path. There are rabbit warrens and runs, small groughs, bogs and small potholes to contend with. No side of the hill offers an easy route up excepting maybe the western flank from the bridle path above Carr Meadow. This area is widely used during the shooting season, so watch out for the notices posted at access points.

Upon reaching the summit it is nice to look around and reflect on all the fine views from here. It may only be 1400ft. high (454m) but I would put it on a par with South Head for the panoramic views. I especially like it in the winter when everything around is crisp and white, gleaming in the winter sunshine. The snowcapped north-west buttress of Kinder when viewed from The Knot seems to rise and stand majestically like one of the Munros of Scotland; a last bastion from civilisation. Other sights to behold from here include Bleaklow, Burnt Hill, Leygatehead Moor, Mill Hill, the north-west to the south-west sweep of Kinder Scout, Lantern Pike and Cown Edge Rocks.

THE LADIE BROOK/CLOUGH END (see Ladyclough)
THE LAND (see Lands Barn)
THE LEE (see Lee Estate)
THE LOVERS (see Win Hill)
THE MILNE HILL (see Mill Hill)

THE NAB GR.125866
Formerly called Oken Nabbe (1659). Found in the parish of Edale above Ollerbrook Clough, this is one of those hills that are only small in stature but present one of those stiff undulating climbs up to the summit. Over the years the hill has started to erode, and because of this sections have been bypassed with new paths and steps. Please use these paths, not just to help ease the erosion, but also for your own safety as well. The summit is slightly rock strewn but rather flat and because it is flat, in the summer months it becomes something of a picnic area for the family day-trippers. Splendid views from here of The Great Ridge, the vale below, Grindsbrook Clough and the escarpment of the rocky Ringing Roger.

THE PAGODA GR.088870
Basically this very fine rock formation is the start of the Woolpacks on its western flanks. Lying to the right of the Pym Chair the shape of The Pagoda represents slab upon slab of huge rocks which rise up and gradually taper off to a flat top.

THE ROACHE CLOUGHE AND THE ROCH CLOUGH (see Roych Clough)
THE ROCHE (see The Roych)
THE ROICHE CLOUGH (see Roych Clough)
THE ROUCHE FIELD (see The Roych)
THE ROUGHE BANCK (see Rough Bank)

THE ROYCH (1704) GR.075845
Another of those areas that God in all his wisdom chose to create as a bog squelching morass, and it is just as well that this land lies within the no access area. The Roych in its prime farming days, was (and still is to a certain degree) enclosed within four large dry-stone walls. The terrain is criss-crossed with feeders for the brook in the Roych Clough.

The land is also steepish; not ideal land for farming.

THE RUNGE GR.076884
A long lost name for the area where the confluence of the River Kinder and Red Brook meet just above Peter Nook Wood. I find it one of the most tranquil spots of the lower regions of Kinder on this side, for here you can have solitude and quietness broken only by the cascading river and the miniature waterfalls which create deep pools. In winter the scenery takes on a new lease of life with the waterfalls freezing up and the grasses and small shrubs trapped in cocoons of ice.

THE SEELE EDGE (see Seal Edge)

THE TIPS GR.105844
Not a refuse area for household garbage, but an area where many little humps are to be found, made up of the waste slag, earth and stone from the workings of the Cowburn Tunnel. The deposited waste built up and can still be seen today, though the humps have become overgrown now. They can be found at the Edale end of the tunnel. Access is gained via either Upper or Barber Booth and then across to Dalehead.

THE TIPS HAUNTING GR.105844
The locals tell of a black collie dog that haunts The Tips, occasionally heard, though very, very rarely seen. Nobody seems to know why it should haunt this area or where it came from.

THE WICKEN GR.126892
Formerly called Whickes (1629) and Whiken Cloughe (1637). Close by the Blackden Barn this area falls just within the open access boundary, and once boasted a fine wood. Alas, it lies almost bare now except for a sparse bush here and there. The remains of the wood can be located on the banks of the River Ashop in the Woodlands Valley. There are not a lot of trees left and they are out-of-bounds anyway, for this area round the river is private.

THOMASON'S HOLLOW (1817) GR.096927
This place was named after a gentleman called John Thomason who lived in 1635. It is a very pleasant place when the sun is shining, though at any other time it is not very appealing. The name is misleading for it is less of a hollow and more of a clough whose brook has a small waterfall flowing off the peat-sodden Salvin Ridge. The

brook then tumbles into the pleasant and picturesque Lady Clough, lying in the shadows of the Snake Pass Road, opposite Doctor's Gate Culvert.

THORN BUSH HILL, THORNELL AND THORN HILL
(see Kinder Parishes)

THORNHILL BRINK GR.180851
No thorny problems here for there are no thorns of any description! The name applies to a ridge, the first/last ridge of the Kinder Massif, which links up with the Hope Brink and the splendid Win Hill Pike. Only two problems seem to bother the backpacker along this ridge, firstly the wind, for it always seems to whip across here, and secondly in winter when the ridge tends to become an icy glacier making walking very hazardous. One or two paths lead off from the ridge to the banks of the Ladybower Reservoir.

THORNHILL CARR FOOTPATH GR.195851
An alternative but longer route that takes the strain out of going up the Yorkshire Bridge Track via Parkin Clough. To gain access to the Carr footpath you must pass the entrance to Parkin Clough just past the Yorkshire Bridge, and carry on up the narrow road till you come to the Ladybower Dam. From here you can follow the path round on the banks of the reservoir and take any of the numerous left-hand slip tracks. These small tracks will take you up through the conifer plantation. All these minor tracks come out at some point on the Thornhill Carr footpath. When this path has been attained turn to your left and follow the Thornhill Carr path upwards - eventually it will cross Parkin Clough some threequarters of the way up the clough. From this point it is but a short walk up the rest of Parkin Clough to Winhill Pike. If you decide not to go up the rest of Parkin Clough then you may carry on walking the Thornhill Carr footpath to either Ashton or Thornhill. The choice is yours.

THORNHULLE (see Kinder Parishes)

THREE KNOLLS GR.071871
Formerly Three Knowles (1829). The name refers to three distinct humps, which are slightly rocky, lying below Kinderlow and above Broad Clough. Viewed from certain angles the humps resemble some sort of gigantic monster, which appears to be laying down. So tread quietly along the path over the humps so as not to disturb its slumber!

THREE KNOWLES (see Three Knolls)
THUNDERBOLT P47C (see Kinder Aircraft Crash Sites)
THURNHILL (see Kinder Parishes)
TIN TOWN (see Kinder Village)
TIP THE DOG (see Yorkshire Bridge)
TOBOGGAN RUN (see Ski Run)

TOM HEYS (1714) GR.035897 THE INTAKES (1830) GR.034900
Tom Heys is the place name of a smallholding close by Carr Meadow. Behind the small farm is to be found an old well and the remains of some long lost quarries. These lead us into the Intakes, formerly called the Intacke (1577); a very marshy area leading up to Burnt Hill.

TOOT HILL GR.085837
Another hill technically out-of-bounds to the backpacker, though initially there are the odd one or two faint paths over this hill. The paths mainly connect Roych Tor and clough with Colborne and Horsehill Tor. The summit of the hill lies over the direct line of the Cowburn Tunnel. The air shaft of the tunnel cannot be missed for it resembles a square castle turret.

TRIANGULATION STATIONS/TRIG POINTS
(see Ordnance Survey Pillars)

TUNSTEAD CLOUGH (1829) GR.055868
The upper half of this clough lies within the boundary of the National Trust, however you will find entry into this clough legally impossible for there are notices at strategic points warning people to keep out. From the footbridge over the brook, lying in the shadows of the old Tunstead farmhouse, the clough looks quite serene in the evening sunshine when the tree laden clough casts long shadows along the ground. The brook which flows down off Broad Clough is a main feeder for the River Sett, which it meets at the infamous Terror Bridge at the base of the clough.

TUNSTEAD FARM AND GUEST HOUSE GR.054867
These two buildings date back nearly three hundred years, and stand in the shape of a letter 'L'. The farm was extensively used in the 17th and 18th centuries as a resting house for travellers and traders leading their packhorses over the ancient bridle paths between the villages and towns of Castleton, Edale, Hayfield and Glossop. Spare horses could also be obtained here. The farm has changed little over the years, the

only exception being that in 1925, the house next to the farm opened its doors to anyone wanting to stay the night. Previous to this ramblers had often called here for a cool refreshing drink, so the owners, using a bit of initiative, opened up as a guest house, where it still thrives to this day.

TURNHULL (see Kinder Parishes)
TYM, MIKE (see Four Jacks Cabin)

—U—

UPPER ASHOP GR.143892
A smallholding lying on the slopes of Blackley Hey in the Woodlands Valley, which overlooks the River Ashop and the Snake Road. This is a private area but paths, including the course of a roman road do skirt around the holding, to or from the Rowlee Bridge.

UPPER BOOTH (1732) GR.104854
A picturesque booth lying in the shadows of Crowden Clough within the parish of Edale. Depending on the direction you are travelling with a vehicle, the booth is either the start or the end of the main thoroughfare through the Vale of Edale. There are no car parking spaces at the booth itself, though there is midway between it and Barber Booth. From Upper Booth it is all leg work: the Pennine Way route via Jacob's Ladder passes this way. A curio of this farming hamlet is the small postbox set into the wall of the stables in the farmyard.

UPPER GATE CLOUGH GR.092910
A small clough situated on the wild Featherbed area, which leads down into the Ashop Clough valley, crossing the Snake Path before emptying its contents into the River Ashop. There is a fairly steep climb up the clough to the Featherbed and Salvin Ridge summit. However, this is compensated for by the meandering and often cascading brook over the very stony bed.

UPPER HOUSE (1829) GR.063878
Originally called Higher House, and was built when the surrounding area would have been quite thickly wooded, with a natural basin lying below. The years passed with the house changing hands now and again and the land face changing dramatically. A certain James Watt purchased the house after securing Farlands close by, and he set about

converting it into a picturesque manor house, with a drive sweeping through magnificent gardens to a clock tower, archways and court-yards. Whilst this was in progress, the sister house of Upper House, Lower House, which rested in the basin below, was being submerged under Kinder Reservoir.

To view this fine example of 17th century workmanship I suggest taking the Farlands to Broad Clough footpath, where midway you will overlook this splendid sprawling house, set in and surrounded by towering conifer trees.

UPPER MOOR, EDALE GR.140873

Located on the far south-eastern upper regions of the Scout's plateau; a foreboding place on a wet and misty day. The terrain here is riddled with peat hags but it is the peat pools which hold the danger: nowhere else on the plateau are there so many concentrated in such a small area. In general a desert of hidden danger, so tread warily on crossing. In contrast, the fringes are not too bad for there are one or two minor paths which skirt around the edges of the moor.

UPPER MOOR, HAYFIELD GR.064878

Formerly called More (1346), Heyfield Moor (1640) and Hayfield Moor (1830). This must have caused some confusion to the locals, for these names were also used to describe Middle Moor which overlooks Hayfield. How different Upper Moor is from its namesake over in Edale, for this is a most scenic area where the boundary of open access runs directly over the top. Access has been kindly allowed by the estate of Upper House, so backpackers please note and respectfully keep to the paths.

UPPER RED BROOK (1840) GR.080902

A trickle more than a brook in the summer months, which makes its way from off the Kinder Edge and then meanders on down through the Black Ashop Moor to feed the River Ashop. To walk up the clough is quite steady going until you reach the base of the escarp-ment, where it becomes very rocky and the going gets hard.

UPPER SEAL CLOUGH (see Seal Flats)

UPPER TOR GR.116876

This tor is the companion of the Far Upper and Nether Tors, overlooking the splendid valley of Grindsbrook Clough. Viewed from the clough the tor rises magnificently, making a splendid scenic escarpment. The tor is also famous for its rock climbing, but like its companions, this tor is also subject to erosion.

UPPER WESTERN BUTTRESS GR.070895
Whimsically known as The Armchair from its shape. A lofty escarpment often used as a rock climbing area, suitable for all grades of climbers. The terrain around the base is boulder strewn and this stretches around to the foot of Sandy Heys. The views from the summit are very good and from here you can take in a splendid view of the Mermaid's Pool. Experienced climbers who tire of this buttress can amble but a short distance to the amphitheatre of rocks at the Kinder Downfall.

URCHIN CLOUGH (see Rough Bank. Formerly Urchin Clough Head)

—V—

VALE OF EDALE GR.088862 - 163364
The Vale is approximately 6 miles (9kms.) long, stretching from the foot of Jacob's Ladder then winding its way through Edale to Edale End, overshadowed by Lose Hill and the Hope Brink. Some quaint hamlets-cum-booths enchant the Vale, where it seems in certain places that they have been untouched by modern methods and techniques. Mind you, the scenery in the vale has changed dramatically over the centuries, for in the days of old when the land was ruled by petty kings and their wise men and wizards, the vale was thickly overgrown with a huge forest, inhabited by the bear, wild boar, mountain cats and the big bad wolf. Nowadays it is quite safe to walk through the vale, excepting for the odd wreckless road hog to contend with.

The railway arrived at Edale in 1894 and since then the population of the vale has seen a steady decrease. The locals seemed to be waiting for some sort of transport to get them out of the valley into civilisation - or into the rat race. Today there is a very limited train service, and no bus service. However, the vale can be reached quite easily on foot in comfort and in plenty of time for the return trip from any of the following points: Hayfield, Castleton, Hope, Hathersage, Bamford, Chinley, Chapel-en-le-Frith and Bradwell.

VALLEY OF THE RIVER (see Edale)
VALLEY OF THE RUNNING STREAM (see Edale)

—W—

WAINWRIGHT, ALFRED
More generally associated with the fells of the Lake District, Alfred Wainwright has played his part in familiarizing people with the terrain of Kinder through his excellent book, *Pennine Way Companion*. The detail and information he has packed into this book makes it invaluable to anyone attempting this classic walk.

WAMSBROW (see Broad Clough)
WARD, HUMPHREY (see David Grieve)
WATER OVER THE EDGE (see Kinder Downfall)

WATERSIDE CARAVAN AND CAMPING SITE GR.118849
Formerly called Waterside Farm (1840). Very near to Barber Booth in the Vale of Edale stands a small cluster of holdings facing the River Noe. This area comes under the name of Waterside and represents a place where backpackers can rent a caravan or pitch a tent. You could not wish to wake up to a better view, for facing you there is The Great Ridge, with Mam Tor and Rushup Edge looking down upon you.

WATT, JAMES (see Farlands and Upper House)
WATT, MATTHEW (see Farlands)
WELLINGTON BOMBER (see Kinder Aircraft Crash Sites, two references)
WHICKES AND WHIKEN CLOUGH (see The Wicken)
WHIPSNADE (see Woolpacks)

WHITE BROW (1829) GR.055883
Situated on the western side of the Kinder Reservoir where conservation work has been carried out on repairing and renewing the footpaths at the base of the brow. The brow is easily accessible via Hayfield or from Carr Meadow over Middle Moor. There are fine views from here of the reservoir sections of the Kinder Amphitheatre leading up to the Kinder Downfall.

WHITEHORN CLOUGH GR.047913
A long, steep, winding clough on the eastern side of Shaw Moor overlooked by the Worm Stones. The name is derived from its upper regions which is all shaley and has become bleached white by the elements. A shooting cabin stands about halfway down its eastern bank overlooking the clough.

WHITE LADY GR.054863
Not an apparition as the name seems to imply, but a large standing stone on the Coldwell Clough Road, overlooking and facing The Ashes. On the face of the stone is a small hole which looks directly onto the Ashes Farm. When viewed through this hole at night the farm is supposed to appear to move from side to side! If you should witness this do not tell anyone or they may carry you off to a secure place!

WHITEMOORLEY BOOTH, WHITEMORELEY AND WHITMORLIE BOOTH (see Barber Booth)

WILLIAM CLOUGH (1840) GR.078910
This clough was named after a miner back in the medieval days, who had a smelting works close by the clough. William the Smith was his name and even today you may chance across some very small pockets of slag around this area.

The summit lies on the flat land between the north-western buttress of Kinder and Mill Hill, whilst the base, an outlet for the brook, emerges at the northern tip of the Kinder Reservoir. In between the base and the summit lies a steep, meandering and in places rocky path, where care is needed for at certain points it is very suspect to erosion. In winter the path can become very treacherous and on more than one occasion I have foresaken the path and come down the brook itself.

WILLIAM THE SMITH (see William Clough)

WIN HILL - PIKE GR.187851
Former names are Wythinehull in the 13th century and Winnehill (1566). The first or last bastion of the Kinder Massif. From the summit of this small but significant hill, which resembles a volcano from afar, you can take in splendid views of a large slice of the High Peak. The 360° sweep takes in the rocky escarpment of Bamford Edge, standing defiantly on the ede of Bamford Moor which in its turn is overlooked by the magical Stanage Edge. Farther round and lying below, you can take in the picturesque Hope Valley along with the charming Vale of Edale, whilst above these two valleys runs the Great Ridge, separating the limestone and gritstone lands. Overshadowing the Great Ridge stands the massif and rugged Kinder, challenging all to come and conquer it. Below you stretches the tall conifers of the thickly wooded Woodlands Valley, surrounded by the towering

moors, which in turn encase the man-made Lakes of the Peak, the Ladybower and Derwent Reservoirs. All in all, this is one of the finest viewpoints of the High Peak.

The hill itself is steeped in legends and folklore. Legend says that Win Hill derives its name from long ago in Saxon Britain, when a battle was fought in the Hope Valley between two armies, the Northumbrians and an army from Wessex. The two armies were camped on two hills facing each other and these were named after the victors and losers; hence we have Win Hill whilst opposite we have Lose Hill, the start of the Great Ridge. The Northumbrians won incidentally!

The summit is capped by an Ordnance Survey pillar, close to the site of an old exhumed grave of two lovers. There is a strange tale about the two lovers, who were found together, dead, on Win Hill itself, and were mysteriously buried there. There they remained for twenty years until it was decided to have them exhumed. When the bodies were uncovered they were both found to be in perfect condition, with no deterioration whatsoever. They were reburied in the same spot, and another twenty years elapsed before the same ritual took place again. As before, the two lovers were found to be in perfect condition, so for a third time they were buried and twenty years after they were once again exhumed, only to be found as perfectly preserved as ever. This time, however, the two lovers were moved to the Hope churchyard and reburied. A few more years elapsed when once again it was decided to exhume the lovers, but this time when the grave was opened, the two bodies had completely decomposed. Or had they, as some locals of the time thought, returned to their beloved Win Hill?

WINHILL PLANTATION GR.192850

Basically the southern tip of the Woodlands Valley Forest, it is here after the gruelling climb up the tiring Yorkshire Bridge Track via Parkin Clough that you get a little respite. The path continues up from the clough through the sparse plantation, but the going becomes a lot easier and this can put you in a better frame of mind for the last leg onto the summit of Win Hill.

WISEMAN HEY CLOUGH PLANTATION (1850) GR.180858

Another conifer plantation which is also swallowed up in the forest of the Woodlands Valley. The plantation lies on the northern slopes of Win Hill and descends down to the banks of the Ladybower Reservoir, where a number of paths are to be found that pass through the plantation in various directions. Please keep to these paths and respect the land.

WITHIN CLOUGH (1627) GR.080915
A very long and meandering clough which starts its journey on the wild and barren Featherbed Moss, not very far from the Snake Pass summit. Surprisingly it is one of the few cloughs on and around Kinder that is almost rock free. It winds its way down into the Ashop Valley where the brook from the clough marries up with the River Ashop, and it is at this point after heavy rain that the Snake Path can become quite boggy.

WOLVE HILL (see Wove Hill)
WOLVELOUE (see Wooler Knoll)
WOODLAND AND WOODLAND HAMLET
(see Kinder Parishes)
WOODLANDS DALE (see Woodlands Valley)

WOODLANDS VALLEY GR.113906 - 180860
Formerly called the Woodlands Dale (1840). The valley starts in the vicinity of the Snake Inn and ends at the water catchment of the Ladybower Reservoir, via the A54 Snake Road. The length of the valley is in the region of 5 miles (8kms.) and was at one time in its life a very heavily wooded region. Alas, this is not so now, though the Forestry Commission have tried over the years to rectify this. The most densely populated areas are now the start and finish of the valley, whilst trees are sparse in the middle section. There is only a handful of farming communities along the valley. The only means of transport is by car for there is no call for a bus service, and the nearest rail link is over the Scout at Edale; a fair walk for anybody. Apart from these drawbacks the valley is pleasant enough to amble along, with scenic views of the north-eastern flanks and moors of Kinder.

WOODHOUSE GR.135861
So named because this small farming community lies in the shadow of a wood, somewhat smaller in its size than when Woodhouse was first built. The access point for the Rowland Cote Moor. The Youth Hostel lies at the back of the farm.

WOOD MOOR GR.120894
Sandwiched between Seal Flats and the Wicken, this moor is not what its name seems to imply, a wooded moor - not nowadays anyway, though it used to be a few hundred years ago. Now there is not a single

tree.

WOOLER KNOLL (1840) GR.172863
Formerly Wolveloue (1285) and Woolowe (1599). The name originates from wolf, for in medieval times this area was known to be a favourite haunt of wolves.

The knoll is very small and is not easy to locate for it lies on the upper fringes of the forest in the Woodlands Valley, close by the Hope Brink. If it wasn't for the surrounding woodland the view from the top of the knoll would be similar to that from Win Hill.

WOOLPACKS (1809) GR.090868
Also known by two other names though both are little used: Whipsnade or - aptly - Mushroom Garden. This area is made up of a large outcrop of amazing abstract rocks formations, many mushroomed shape, hence the name. The most famous of the rocks are Pym Chair and the Pagoda, but there are many many more. Couple the Woolpacks in a walk with Crowden Tower and you can spend a pleasant two or three hours exploring and examining these rocks which have stood here for millions of years. If you are fond of photography you will have a field day amongst these rocks, especially if there is a slight mist swirling about which gives them a haunting aura.

WORM STONES (see Shaw Moor)

WOVE HILL GR.103884
Also known as Wolve Hill, as the name is derived from wolf as was Wooler Knoll. The hill is situated out on the plateau and around its base can be found the wreckage of a Dragon Rapide. Sitting upon the summit rocks of the hill by yourself, you gain a sense of freedom combined with solitude, for all around you lies bare the barren plateau.

WYTHINEHULL (see Win Hill)

—X Y Z—

YEMAN'S BRIDGE GR.127853
This old stone bridge carries the main road through the Vale of Edale. Formerly a wooden bridge was situated here, but it was called Yeomansfields (1707) and Yeoman Field (1840). During the summer weekends the bridge carries considerable traffic, due mainly to

tourists and trippers whilst the rest of the time it is mainly quiet and tranquil. There are some very fine views from here, most notably The Great Ridge where Man Tor stands and gazes out over the vale.

YEOMAN FIELD AND YEOMANSFIELD (see Yeman's Bridge)

YONGATE OR YONGATE BRIDGE GR.088862

A very old packhorse bridge than spans the main tributary of the River Noe at the foot of Jacob's Ladder. The bridge has been repaired and strengthened over the last few years, whilst the general area here has had a face lift. (see Jacob's Ladder)

YORKESHIRE BRIDGE AND YORKESHIRE BRIGG (see Yorkshire Bridge)

YORKSHIRE BRIDGE GR.198849

Prior to the construction of this double arched bridge which spans the River Derwent there used to be a wooden bridge, formerly called Yorkeshire Bridge (1599) and Yorkeshire Brigg (1687). The present bridge was constructed in 1695 and at the time was the last packhorse bridge before the border into Yorkshire. The carved stone pillars at the end of the bridge originated from the old Derwent Hall, which used to stand in the Derwent Valley, now occupied by the northern water catchment of the Ladybower Reservoir.

Close by the bridge there is a holding where 'Tip', the devoted dog of Joseph Tagg, lived with his master, and a small memorial stone by the side of the Derwent Dam commemorates Tip's devotion.

Upon crossing the Yorkshire Bridge from the Bamford side you now enter Kinderland, where the first big obstacle confronts you, the Yorkshire Bridge Track via Parkin Clough: the first hill to climb of the Kinder Massif.

YORKSHIRE BRIDGE TRACK (see Parkin Clough)

YOUTH HOSTELS OR HOSTELS

There are three hostels in the proximity of Kinder, the furthest one being in Castleton. The other two are more centralised for Kinder, one being at Edale, the Rowland Cote Youth Hostel already mentioned, and the other hostel can be found off the Snake Road opposite Blackley Hey; Hagg Farm. Apart from the hostels there are many places for accommodation in the area.

90 *The undulating frozen maze of groughs on the central plateau of Kinder Scout.*

THE KINDER AIRCRAFT CRASH SITES

There have been numerous aircraft crashes in the Peak District, of which Kinder has had its fair share. Quite a few of the crashes happened before and during the second world war. Mystery still surrounds certain crashes, questions on how and why they crashed remain unanswered, only theories have been put forward.

As previously stated, no wreckage of any description may be removed without prior consent from the Ministry of Defence.

The following crash sites all relate to Kinder itself.

1937 JULY 22nd

HANDLEY PAGE HEYFORD

GR.112862 BROADLEE BANK TOR

The Handley Page Heyford was designed as a heavy night bomber. This particular aircraft, Heyford K6875 of 166 Squadron was on a flying exercise from its aerodrome in Leconfield near Beverley, Yorkshire. At approximately 11.00pm. on July 22nd 1937 there were reports of flares being fired from the plane, which at the time was flying at a low altitude down the dark Vale of Edale, some 14 to 15 degrees off course. The Heyford blanked and started circling when at precisely 11.00pm. it mysteriously crashed upon the summit of Broadlee Bank Tor. The crew of six must have died a horrible death for the plane burst into flames and was completely gutted.

The unanswered questions are: Why was the aircraft flying so low in a mountainous region and why was the Heyford so far off course!

1941 JULY 31st

WELLINGTON W5719

GR.111877 FAR UPPER TOR

Only tiny fragments remain of this Wellington Bomber, which crashed in the Grindsbrook Valley. This particular bomber, one of eight that took off from Snaith, Yorkshire, was to take part in a bombing raid over Cologne. The planes took off in atrocious weather conditions which persisted all the way to the target. However, with conditions being so bad only five of the Wellingtons actually reached Cologne, where they discharged their bomb load. Two of the remaining three planes found other targets over Belgium, whilst the remaining bomber, Wellington W5719 of 150 Squadron, had run into an extremely bad storm. Unable to bypass it in any way, the pilot, Sergeant Parrot, decided to return to base. Matters were made worse when the Navigator, a Canadian, named Sergeant Evelle, informed the crew that the storm had cut out the radio.

A few estimated calculations led the Navigator to believe they had reached the Home Coast in the area of the Wash. Cloud was still very low and dense, but Sergeant Parrot must have believed that he was near to Snaith for he dropped extremely low through the thick cloud hoping for a landmark. What he saw would literally have turned his stomach, for he had dropped into Grindsbrook Clough with the towering rocky escarpments of the three tors facing him. He had no chance to pull out or gain altitude. The Wellington smashed into the Far Upper Tor where the plane, still carrying its full bomb load of 3,500lbs. disintegrated. All excepting the rear turret occupied by the Rear Gunner, Sergeant Earl Tilley, another Canadian, was blown off in the ensuing explosion. Sergeant Tilley was the only survivor. The others, Sergeant Parrot, Second Pilot Sergeant Haswell, Wireless Operator Sergeant Webber and Sergeant Evelle would have been killed outright.

In 1984, on the summit of Far Upper Tor, somebody had gone to the trouble to make a little shrine. It was made out of fragments from the Wellington with a small cross placed above. On the cross was a little medal with the Squadron's insignia. A small plaque was also at hand with an inscription reminding us of the dead airmen of Wellington W5719.

Alas! there remains nothing of this now; somebody may have remove it for some reason, or the weather may have dislodged it; the memory blown away in the strong Peak winds.

1942 MARCH 21st

HAMPDEN BOMBER AE381
GR.078875 CLUTHER ROCKS

The bomber, piloted by an inexperienced crew of Australians, were on a cross-country exercise from Skellingthorpe, a small rural area not far from Lincoln. Due to the inexperience of the crew they found themselves some 40 to 50 miles (60 to 70kms.) off course and completely lost. They managed to get in touch with the control tower at Ringway Airport, Manchester, and instructions were relayed to the crew about the landing procedure. There was doubt as to whether the runway could be seen clearly in the adverse weather conditions, but the bomber was set on its course and it approached the runway from the east. It came in low but overshot the runway, passing on into the distance. The Wireless Operator at Ringway was informed by the police at Hayfield that the bomber had crashed into the hillside above Kinder Reservoir. There were no survivors.

No wreckage is to be found at the scene of the crash - north-west of the Kinder Low Ordnance Survey pillar.

1943 JANUARY 26th

WELLINGTON BOMBER X3348
GR.129877 BLACKDEN EDGE

Eight Wellington Bombers from 427 Squadron had been on a bombing raid over France, but due to the distance and time spent on the bombing run, fuel was getting low. Instructions were relayed to the pilots to land and refuel at any airfield available. One by one the planes landed at various airfields, with one plane actually reaching its home base of Croft, North Yorkshire.

The pilot of Wellington X3348, unsure of his whereabouts, came down through the cloud, only to discover the plateau of Kinder Scout. Fuel was now at critical level, so Pilot Officer Carl Taylor decided on a forced landing. He relayed this to his co-pilot Sergeant Southward, who was flying the plane, and Southward brought it down rather well considering the terrain he was forced to land on. Fate must have smiled on the crew for there were no serious injuries and the plane was more or less in one piece.

The plane was stripped and dismantled then taken off to the scrap-yard. A few fragments remain, the most concentrated area being about a hundred paces south east of Blackden Edge Ordnance Survey pillar.

1943 APRIL 25th (EASTER SUNDAY)

THUNDERBOLT P47C
GR.093854 HORSEHILL TOR

Another crash where the weather played a major role, this time not so tragically. The story starts early on Easter Sunday April 25th 1943, where Second Lieutenant John E.Coenen of 63 Fighter Squadron USAAF, 8th Airforce, 56 Fighter Group, stationed at Horsham St. Faith, not far from Norwich, volunteered to fly to Liverpool to pick up some spare parts. The plane he was to fly was a Thunderbolt P47C, a fighter plane which was rather clumsy looking and was consequently nicknamed a 'Jug'. He took off into a very heavy wind but the journey to Liverpool proved to be just a normal flight. He landed without trouble but then discovered that he would be delayed in getting the parts he had come for. After a great deal of chasing around he acquired the necessary parts, but this had now brought him to the early evening, and the weather had taken a turn for the worse. As the pilot took off there was thick cloud now covering the hills. Second Lieutenant Coenen made up his mind to take the plane high above the cloud. He started his ascent when all of a sudden the Thunderbolt got caught up in some kind of turbulence, resulting in the pilot losing all control and sense of direction. Unexpectedly the plane started to lose height and it fell into a spin. Coenen, having no chance to pull out of the spin, hurriedly pushed back his cockpit canopy and attempted to bale out. For some reason he found he could not jump out, but then, unexpectedly, he was literally torn out of the cockpit when his ripcord was released. Glancing up at his chute he noticed that there was a large rent in it, also a small piece was missing, and this resulted in Coenen descending too fast. He hit the ground rather badly and was dragged along by his chute. Luckily he was spotted coming down and help was at hand in a matter of minutes. In hospital it was found that he had sustained injuries to his vertebrae. However, within five months he was back in action, though he was eventually grounded because the injuries he sustained impeded his control when flying aircraft. As to the Thunderbolt, this crashed onto Horsehill Tor not far from the Boundary Stone. There is little left of the plane now.

1943 OCTOBER 5th

HALIFAX HR727

GR.129879 BLACKDEN EDGE

It seems uncanny that within nine months two planes should crash five minutes' walking distance from each other, when you consider the amount of high ground there is in the Dark Peak. Unlike the January crash, which involved a Wellington when no lives were lost, Blackden Edge this time only spared two of the seven man crew of the Halifax Bomber. Officially the records state that Flight Engineer Eric Lane was chiefly responsible for the crash, for not keeping a check on the fuel that was left in the plane's tanks, though a small part of the blame was put onto the Pilot. Evidence seems to indicate that a number of factors contributed to the crash, though these were never officially recorded.

The crew of the Halifax was made up as follows:- Pilot Ernie Fenning, Wireless Operator Sergeant Frank Squibbs, Navigator G.Forth (a Canadian), Bomb Aimer Sergeant Victor Garland. Mid-Upper Gunner Sergeant Short, Engineer E.Lane and Rear Gunner Sergeant J.Mack.

They took off in the Halifax HR727 from Snaith, Yorkshire on a reasonably calm evening, along with the rest of the task force, heading for Frankfurt. At approximately 9.25pm. the bombers reached their target, HR727 released its own 4,500lb. bomb load along with the other bombers. Frankfurt now became a blazing inferno, which was to burn for 60 hours continuously. Their bomb run now over, the Halifax HR727 turned for home but flew smack into flak and the sweeping searchlights. Then from above them appeared a flight of Messerschmitt 110's, one of which broke off to engage HR727. Pilot Fenning managed to outmanoeuvre the Messerschmitt but unfortunately the plane had been hit in one of its main fuel tanks; this was noted by Engineer Lane who then relayed it through to the Pilot.

Problems started to arise when they reached the home coast, because fuel was now at a critical stage. Only one engine was being used to try and even out the fuel tanks. The radio packed up at a crucial stage, just as the weather had taken a turn for the worse with strong winds and torrential rain, which made the sighting of familiar territory or landmarks impossible. Pilot Officer Fenning knew that time and fuel was running out fast. He relayed to his crew that he was going down, but the plane never started its descent because it was already below 2,000 feet. It smashed into Blackden Edge, disintegrating over a wide area. Four of the crew were killed outright; Fenning, Forth, Squibbs and Short. Mack was alright and he located Lane who appeared to have no external injuries, though Lane insisted he was hurting badly. Mack left him whilst he went looking for Garland, who was injured around the feet and ankles. Mack decided to go for help. With the weather being so poor it took the rescue team ten hours to locate the wreckage. Of the two men left at the wreckage, Lane had died of massive internal bleeding.

Why did the records blame the Chief Engineer, when a number of factors contributed to the fate of the Halifax HR727?

Not a great deal remains of the wreckage and what there is has been gathered up into a small heap by people who care.

1944 DECEMBER 11th

ANSON N9853

GR.101878 EDALE MOOR

This is the only crash in the Kinder area that involves a contingent of Polish airmen. There were six on board the Avro Anson; three were Pilot Instructors en route for Millom in Cumberland and a fourth was going to inspect some new American equipment. This left the crew of two, the Wireless Operator and the Pilot, Flight Lieutenant Chelstowski, who after the crash was blamed for the catastrophe, despite the fact that the altimeter installed in the Anson was of the old

Mk I type, which allowed a deficit of 500 feet - ridiculous when flying in low cloud over mountainous regions.

The Anson took off from the 16 Service Flying Training School, Newton, Nottinghamshire en route with its passengers for Millom. All went well until the Peak District was reached where once again adverse weather conditions were met: this time the thick cloud was accompanied by swirling snow. The Anson dropped down to 2,500 feet, according to the altimeter, but this could have had a deficit of 500 feet, so in actual fact the plane was only at a height of 2,000 feet; too low for the Peak. The plane hit the barren, bumpy, Edale Moor, finishing up on its back. There were four casualties, two of which were serious. One of the two uninjured airmen went for help down in Edale, where four hours after the crash a rescue party saw to the ministrations of the injured airmen. In due time all the injured recovered - in fact, all six survived the war.

There is a small amount of wreckage about, which is located south-west of the ruins of the Four Jacks Cabin more or less in line with the Dragon Rapide crash site.

1945 NOVEMBER 23rd

Mk XI LIGHT TRANSPORT ANSON

GR.091866 THE CLOUGHS

A tragic story lies behind this unfortunate crash. This particular aircraft, Anson NL185 had been stripped of all the radio equipment from the cockpit, the aircraft was to be then transferred from its base of Halton, a village just south-east of Aylesbury, Buckinghamshire, to Feltwell. This was an airfield near the fens of Norfolk. The total flying distance of the transfer was about 73 miles (110kms.). A flight plan had been carefully worked out for the weather had turned bad and visibility was rather poor. The route to be taken was up towards the east coast of Lincolnshire, turn over the Wash, locate Kings Lynn, then fly due south the last 20 miles (16kms.) to Feltwell.

The Pilot, Wing Commander E.D.Spear, was very experienced with 2,699 flying hours behind him, so this trip should have been a 'piece of cake'. Spear set his compass before taking off, on a bearing which should have read 030 degrees, but the assumption is that Spear inadvertently set his compass on a bearing of 330 degrees instead.

With cloud being so heavy, Spear must have estimated when he was over the Lincolnshire coast. He would have dropped down to 2,000 feet (600m) so that the cloud cover would not be as thick, hoping that he could locate the Wash and make his vital turn to Kings Lynn. What he saw must have turned him inside out; instead of the pleasant

Lincolnshire coast, he would have seen the dark land of the Peak District with the southern buttress looming nearer with every second.

His approximate speed would have been about 150mph. (220kms.). At that speed he had no chance of altering course or gaining height. The Anson smashed into the rocks, causing wreckage to be strewn over a wide area. It was not until the following morning when a farmer's son came across the wreckage, that the Anson, reported missing, presumed lost out over the North Sea was officially crossed off the missing list.

Wing Commander Spear must have been killed outright; a sad end to a distinguished pilot - his ribbons of the D.S.O. and D.F.C. were found on his body.

There is very little now of the wreckage, although an engine can still be seen if you look very carefully in a stream outlet below the Woolpacks.

1945 DECEMBER

LIBERATOR USAAF
GR.058907 MILL HILL

The Liberator had taken part in a massive bombing raid over the Rhine, but due to heavy flak the plane was hit. Turning for home - its base being at Burtonwood - the question on the crew's lips was could they make it home? Lady luck persevered with the limping bomber until fate played its hand, and the bomber was brought down on Mill Hill, breaking up on impact, causing fatalities.

On mist enshrouded days or in inclement weather conditions, certain manifestations have appeared of unfortunate crew members of the Liberator. I have not as yet encountered this phenomenon, but you might - who knows!

There is quite a bit of wreckage. The main bulk of it lies in a large grough, pretty well strung out. Slightly north-east may be found another pile of fragments from the Liberator.

1945 DECEMBER

RAF OXFORD HN594
GR.082852 BROWN KNOLL

This plane crashed onto the summit of Brown Knoll during the winter month of December 1945 in very dense low cloud. There were three men on board the Oxford when the plane had the misfortune to crash, and two of the men suffered serious injury. The third man though injured, managed to crawl and stumble down Brown Knoll to safety. He managed to reach Lee House Farm and cottages, where he told his story. The alarm went out and search parties took to the hills to try to locate and rescue the injured men. This proved impossible because of the mist that completely blanketed the moors, added to which they had no idea where the location of the crashed plane could be. All through the night they searched to no avail, but as dawn broke and the dense mist started to disperse, the RAF sent in planes to search the area. Success was achieved when the wreckage of the Oxford was spotted, and the location was relayed through to the search parties upon the ground who eventually rescued the injured men. They had been lying on the cold, damp and misty moors for almost twenty hours. The identity of the injured man who crawled off for help was Ted Croker; now secretary of the Football Association.

There is very little of the wreckage left now, only fragments here and there around the groughs slightly west of the Brown Knoll Ordnance Survey pillar.

1952 JANUARY 14th

HAVARD FT415

GR.090868 THE CLOUGHS/WOOLPACKS

This particular crash has become one of the strangest mysteries of all the aircraft crashes on Kinder Scout. Once again only theories can be brought forward to ascertain the whys and the wherefores.

Fleet Air Pilot, Midshipman Brian Farley, took off on a south-west bearing on January 14th 1952 on a routine training flight from his base at Syreston Nottingham, down to Kimble Cirencester, a flight of just over one hundred miles. The aircraft was never to arrive at its destination; in fact, to all intents and purposes the plane completely vanished.

On January 19th, five days later, a small party of hikers saw what appeared to be a crashed plane. On closer inspection it proved to be the Harvard, fifty miles off course, broken up and partly gutted with fire. The pilot was still fastened in his cockpit, dead. Why was he flying in a north-westerly direction instead of south-westerly? We shall probably never know the answer.

The pilot of the Harvard was coincidently only about ten miles from his home in Heaton Chapel, Stockport. Had he taken it upon himself to disregard orders and fly over Stockport as a reminder of home, or to picture his hometown from the air?

Wreckage seems to get scarcer each year, for now there remains only a few fragments gathered together in a small pile. These fragments lay in a small hollow. Not far off can be seen the Cheetah engine of an Anson that crashed close by in 1945.

1954 JULY 22nd

SABRES 4's
GR.072902 BLACK ASHOP MOOR

A number of unanswered questions surround the mysterious crash of the two Canadian planes. Sabres XD707 and XD730 had been taking part in an exercise which had involved hundreds of aircraft. The mission of the two Sabres had been quite simple - intercept 'enemy bombers'. The two Sabres had taken off from their base at Linton-on-Ouse, a small village north-west of York, at 5.25pm. with orders to return at 6.25pm. for refuelling. When 6.25pm. arrived no word or sign of acknowledgement had been received - the controllers had tried in vain to contact them via radio. By 6.30pm. the Sabres should be almost out of fuel. Emergency precautions were put into operation, including other civil and military airfields, but no sign had been seen or heard of the missing Sabres.

That same evening two ramblers espied across the Ashop Moor Valley the wreckage of a plane. They immediately returned to inform the police, who in turn informed various search parties from around the area. The search parties found the wreckage of not one plane but two: the missing Sabres. The wreckage was scattered over an extremely wide area of the Ashop Valley and the slopes of Kinder Edge. Both pilots were found to be dead.

A number of questions arise - firstly; why were the Sabres flying so low and 50 miles (80kms.) off course? The pilots had been briefed to fly at 30,000 feet. Secondly; why had no radio contact been established, either to acknowledge base or any other airfield? Thirdly; how did *both* planes come to crash? Fourthly; the biggest mystery of all - one of the pilots had a watch on which had stopped at 7.09pm. -how had the Sabres managed to keep airborne from 6.30pm. to 7.09pm. when fuel should have run out at 6.30pm?

We shall never know all the answers so once again we can only surmise. Firstly, as to flying low, the pilots may have taken it upon themselves to come down low to savour a few minutes before returning to base, but why they should be so far off course and no radio contact defies logical explanation. The crashing may have occurred by the Sabres coming too close to each other in low cloud, resulting in the wings or noses touching. The watch may have been fast or it is possible that it may have been jarred in the ensuing crash. All guesswork...

Parts of the wreckage may still be seen, but it is well strewn out along Black Ashop Moor.

1957 JULY 29th

MILES HAWK

GR.074868 KINDERLOW END

The pilot flying the Miles Hawk G-AJSF, owned by the Blackpool and Fylde Aero Club, was flying the plane from Squire's Gate Airport, Blackpool to Barton Aerodrome near Irlam Manchester. For some reason, perhaps because of low cloud, he passed over Barton and carried on unknowingly towards the Peak District. The plane was seen to suddenly appear out of the low cloud over Kinder Reservoir, heading straight for Kinder Low. It had no sooner appeared when it became engulfed once again in low cloud. The pilot probably never knew what was in front of him, for the plane smacked right into the side of Kinderlow End. The pilot was thrown clear of the cockpit but must have been killed with the impact of the ground.

Why the plane flew on into the Peak District we shall never know.

There is no wreckage, for the plane was completely broken up, and buried at its crash site near to Kinderlow Tumulus.

1963 DECEMBER 30th

DRAGON RAPIDE

GR.102883 WOLVE HILL

The pilot and co-pilot had been carrying out a photographic survey flight in their Dragon Rapide G-ALBC, flying from Middleton St. George near Darlington to Birmingham. However, due to running short on fuel they decided to detour to Ringway Manchester, hoping to refuel there.

After plotting there course they turned for Ringway, the flight path taking them through the Vale of Edale. It was whilst they were flying through the Vale that the Rapide was caught in a sudden down draught, resulting in the plane spinning out of control and finally crashing on Wolve Hill. The co-pilot was flung clear and was only shaken up, whilst the pilot was trapped inside the wreckage with a broken leg. The co-pilot managed to drag him clear and attend to his broken leg as best he could under the circumstances.

With the Rapide overdue, Mountain Rescue Teams were alerted. The pilots were spotted by a helicopter and eventually brought down off the mountain side, very cold but lucky to be alive after their ordeal. The larger part of the Rapide was set on fire and buried at the crash site. There is enough wreckage left to arouse the curiosity of anybody coming across it. To locate the wreckage, from Grindsbrook Towers follow the main brook around to the ruins of the Four Jacks Cabin. Climb up the opposite banking, then on an approximate bearing of north-west lies a rocky knoll and the wreckage is located at the base of this knoll.

Fragments of the Dragon Rapide, Wolve Hill

HANDY QUICK GRID REFERENCES

—A—

Ashop Clough	090907
Ashop Head	066906
Ashop Moor	135885

—B—

Backside Wood	156873
Bagshaw Bridge	162863
Bakestone Delph Clough	054918
Barber Booth	114847
Big & Little Buttress	093898
Black Ashop Moor	090903
Blackden Barn	130894
Blackden Brook	115885
Blackden Edge	132894
Blackden Moor	115885
Blackden Rind	116884
Blackley Clough	155883
Blackley Hey	148888
Black Moor	063923
Black Overhangs	087898
Blackshaws	065883
Blackwall Plantation	132867
Booth	053877
Booths Bridge	052882
Bowden Bridge	050870
Bowden Bridge Quarry	048869
Boxing Glove Stones	078897
Bray Clough	068872
Bridge Chock	085897
Broad Clough	068872
Broadlee Bank Tor	111857
Brown Knoll	084853
Brown Knoll Dyke	084853
Burnt Hill	045902

—C—

Cabin Buttress	096898
Carr House	156866
Carr Meadow	035895
Chendre	087876
Chinese Wall	099891
Chunnal Moor	045905
Clough Farm	146866
Cluther Rocks	078875
Colborne	095837
Coldwell Clough	056859
Coldwell Farm	056859
Coldwell Moor	065858
Cotefield	132860
Cowburn Tunnel	074830 - 105845
Crookstone Barn	157877
Crookstone Hill	150880
Crookstone Knoll	145884
Crookstone Outmoor	143882
Crowden Brook	103858
Crowden Clough	103858
Crowden Head	095882
Crowdenlee Booth	103856
Crowden Tower	095871

—D—

Dalehead	100843
Dean Hill	133890
Dicks Ditch	058857
Dimpus	073854
Dimpus Clough	060850
Dimpus Gate	058847
Doctors Road	045870
Druids Stone	135874
Dry Clough	119875
Dunge Clough	124895

— E —

Edale	125855
Edale Cross	078861
Edale End	163364
Edale Head	085868
Edale Head House	088860
Edale Mill	134854
Edale Moor	095872
Edale Road	050870 - 103854
Edale Rocks	079867

Edale Station	123854
Egg Crag	096897
Elle Bank	048866

—F—

Fair Brook	093892
Fairbrook Naze	096898
Fairbrook Waterfall	093892
Farlands House	053877
Far Upper Tor	110876
Featherbed Moss	085925
Featherbed Top	090921
Fieldhead	125857
Fieldhead Information Centre	124856
Fog Field Well	056861
Four Jacks Cabin	104879
Fox Holes	108871

—G—

Gate Side Clough	118898
Gee Banks	052858
Glead Hill	074915
Golden Clough	122870
Grain Clough	093854
Great Buttress	082888
Grinds Brook	115874
Grindsbrook Booth	123860
Grindsbrook Clough	115874
Grindsbrook Towers	107875
Grindslow House	133864
Grindslow Knoll	110869
Grouse Inn	034905

—H/I—

Harry Hut	045906
Harry Moor	062863
Harts Horn	112879
Hayfield	040868
Hayfield Campsite	048868
Heron Rock/Stone	049870
Highgate	045860
Highmoor Pits	063923
Hill House Farm	052871
Hills House	052871
Holden Clough	073928
Hollingworth Clough	045896
Hollingworth Waterfall	046898
Hollin Head	065886
Hollinshead Farm Remains	065886
Hope Brink	175853
Hope Cross	161857
Horsehill Tor	093848
Hurst Moor	060925

—J—

Jacob's Ladder	087864
Jaggers Clough	145878

—K—

Kinder Amphitheatre	070885
Kinder Bank	047868
Kinder Buttress	078889
Kinder Cavern	073867
Kinder Cottage	052869
Kinder Downfall	082869
Kinder Edge	085898
Kinder Head	060880
Kinder Gates	088887
Kinder Low	079871
Kinderlow Cairn	073867
Kinderlow End	068866
Kinderlow Tumulus	073867
Kinder Plateau	095887
Kinder Printworks	048868
Kinder Reservoir	057887
Kinder Reservoir Mountain Rescue Kit	054882
Kinder Scout	087876
Kinder Summit	087876
Kinder Valley	037869 - 053880
Kinder Valley Mission	051873
Kinder Village	053871
Kirksteads	050871

—L—

Lady Booth	142866
Ladybooth Brook	141865
Lady Clough	096928
Lady Clough Forest	107917
Lady Clough Moor	100921
Lady of the Stairs	052865

Lands Barns	127861
Lee Estate Farmhouse	097856
Leygatehead Moor	055895
Little Hayfield	034882
Lower House	056882

—M—

Madwoman's Stones	138881
Marepiece Wood	051878
Mermaid's Pool	075887
Middle Moor	045885
Middle Seal Clough	112894
Mill Hill	062905
Mill Hill Rocks	067897
Millstones	077877
Misty Buttress	096896
Moss Castle	072916
Mountain Rescue Posts & Kits:-	
Crowden Y.H.	074994
Fieldhead, Edale	124856
Glossop	036943
Kinder Reservoir	054882
Mountain View	052874
Mount Famine	056852

—N—

Nab Brow	058885
Nags Head Inn	124860
Nanny Goat Junction	051872
Nether Booth	142861
Nether Gate Clough	098910
Nether Moor	147875
Nether Ollerbrook	130859
Nether Red Brook	086898
Nether Seal Clough	112894
Nether Tor	124894
Noe Stool	084869
Nungrain Brink	112904
Nungrain Ditch/Dyke	108903

—O—

Oak Bank Cottage	050871
Oaken Clough	068858
Oldpits Plantation	048878
Oller Brook	128862
Ollerbrook Booth	128859
Ollerbrook Clough	128862
Ordnance Survey Pillars:-	
Blackden Edge	129878
Brown Knoll	084851
Harry Hut	045908
Kinder Plateau	078894
Kinder Low	079871
Win Hill	187851
Over Horse Waie	050870 - 103854

—P—

Park Hall	037885
Parkin Clough	196851
Peep O' Day	048850
Peter Nook Wood	070885
Plane Crash Sites:-	
Anson Mk XI	091866
Anson N9853	101878
Dragon Rapide	102883
Halifax	129879
Hampden	078875
Handley Page Heyford	112862
Harvard	090868
Liberator	058907
Miles Hawk	074868
Oxford	082852
Sabres	072902
Thunderbolt	093854
Wellington	129877
Wellington W5719	111877
Pym Chair	088869

—Q/R—

Ramsley Clough	065933
Ramsley Moor	065933
Red Brook	076893
Red Clough	086807
Ridge Wood	154869
Ringing Roger	125873
River Ashop	075907 - 165879
River Edale	084864 - 089861
River Kinder	089884 - 050874
River Noe	088862 - 205825
River Sett	073853 - 001853
Rough Bank	105906
Round Stones	089898

Rowland Cote Moor	134873
Rowland Cote Y.H.	149867
Rowlee Bridge	149891
Roych Clough	080838
Roych Tor	083839

—S—

Salvin Ridge	096920
Sandy Heys	073893
Saukin Ridge	110908
Seal Edge	105887
Seal Flats	112894
Seal Moor	112894
Seal Stones	116887
Seven Minute Crossing	121860
Shaw Moor	044916
Shaw Wood	118854
Shooting Cabins	
Ruins:-	
Ashop Clough	091907
Dry Clough	119875
Dry Clough	119871
Gateside Clough	117893
Span Clough	068925
Swine's Back	076865
Wove Hill	104879
Still in use:-	
Middle Moor	050883
Whitehorn Clough	048913
Ski Run	113868
Slack Barn	158868
Snake Inn	113906
Snake Path	110907 - 041869
Snake Plantation	105915
South Head	061845
Southhead Farm	061855
Span Clough	065928
Span Moor	065928
Spray House/Wood	038892
Stones House	052865
Stonyford	073863
Suave Blocks	092898
Swine's Back	078863

—T—

Tag's Naze	097848
Terror Bridge	053867
The Anvil	084869
The Armchair	070895
The Ashes	055864
The Black Edge	085898
The Cloughs	087866
The Cote	052874
The Edge	085898
The Intakes	034900
The Knot	046894
The Nab	125866
The Pagoda	088870
The Roych	075845
The Runge	076884
The Tips	105844
The Tips Haunting	105844
The Wicken	126892
Thomason's Hollow	096927
Thornhill Brink	180851
Thornhill Carr Footpath	195851
Three Knolls	071871
Tin Town	053871
Toboggan Run	113868
Tom Heys	035897
Toot Hill	085837
Tunstead Clough	055868
Tunstead Farm	054867
Tunstead Guest House	054867

—U—

Upper Ashop	143892
Upper Booth	104854
Upper Gate Clough	092910
Upper House	063878
Upper Moor, Edale	140873
Upper Moor, Hayfield	064878
Upper Red Brook	080902
Upper Seal Clough	112894
Upper Tor	116876
Upper Western Buttress	070895
Urchin Clough	105906

—V—

Vale of Edale	088862 - 163364

View down Blackden Brook, Kinder north.

Fragments of the crashed Harvard plane, The Cloughs/Woolpacks

THE KINDER WALKS

The following routes are designed for the well equipped walker and on no account should they be attempted without a map, compass, whistle, ample food and refreshment and adequate clothing. The walks vary in length, averaging between 10 miles (16 kms.) to 18 miles (28 kms.). The shorter walks are not necessarily the easier or the longest the hardest. All take in a variety of walking conditions and gradients, and one thing you can be sure of is that they will tax your stamina at some point.

The walks all start and finish at some point where public transport is available, but it is advisable to check on the times of buses and trains to get you home, remembering that timetables often have seasonal fluctuations. Some walks start and finish at the same point, and these walks are ideal for the motorist.

You may not choose to do a whole route, preferring to shorten it. Or you could mix-and-match routes up to suite yourself; this is quite feasible with a bit of planning beforehand.

There are no golden rules giving set times for walks or when to rest, but you can reckon on averaging about two miles per hour (three kms.) overall - this allows time for viewing and taking photographs etc. If you can possibly avoid it do not attempt any barren moors or the Kinder Plateau in the heavy snow-laden months, or in thick mists and low cloud, unless you are a very experienced walker with a very good knowledge of the area. In such circumstances you must have a compass, *and know how to use it.* If the elements are against you, turn back or get yourself onto a safe path. There is always another day.

WALK 1 THE EDALE - HAYFIELD VANTAGE POINTS

Length: 10 miles (16 kms.)
Start: Edale Finish:Hayfield
Going: Fairly firm except for one small section
Gradient: Steep at first then very moderate
Time: 6/7 hours with time out for viewing or 4 hours otherwise.

All the walks starting at Edale begin from the station or large car park opposite the station. From the station/car park proceed up the road in the direction of the church passing the Fieldhead Information Centre on your right then the old cemetry opposite the church lying to your left. A short walk from here brings you into Grindsbrook Booth (Edale village). As you face the Old Nag's Head Inn, turn to your left locating the alternative Pennine Way sign and proceed along this route, keeping to it over several stiles whilst you skirt the base of Broadlee Bank Tor. A signpost will come into view midway round the base, which points to the boundary of open access below the base of the tor. Take this route on the base of the tor until on your right-hand side a dry stone wall that is in need of repair, appears and goes directly up the flank of the tor. This is your guide to the summit of the tor; it will not be easy for the route up is extremely steep so prepare yourself. A good rest will not go amiss now that the summit has been attained, so sit down and take in the splendid views to be seen from here.

Ready again, you will now attempt Grindslow Knoll rising in front of you. Walk directly towards its, passing as you do so, two large springs on the plateau of Broadlee Bank Tor. Grindslow Knoll is not as hard to climb as it looks, and within a few minutes you will have attained a large cairn that tops this rocky knoll. You will now have covered 2½ miles (4 kms.) of the walk, and the hardest part. From here you can take in an excellent view of the three tors on the other side of the Grindslow Valley: Far Upper, Upper and Nether Tors. You now turn westwards, locating the path across Edale Moor to the excellent vantage point of Crowden Tower, the 4 mile point (6½ kms.) The going across this moor can be a little sticky at times, but generally the path is firm until you near the summit of Crowden Brook below Crowden Tower where it becomes stickier. After crossing the brook a short walk up the side of the tower will bring you to the flat top and the excellent views of the valley below, most notably Jacob's Ladder.

Turning west again, you carry on along the path into the Mushroom Garden, or to give it its proper name the Woolpacks, where it is advisable to take time out to explore these unusual rock formations. An hour or so which includes refreshment etc. will suffice for the time being, for there is always another day to finish off your exploration.

From the Woolpacks you carry on west with your journey, with your next objective being the large rock called the Noe Stool, but first you must cross a small tract of peat bogs through which the path meanders. As you leave the Woolpacks behind, turn round and look back at them to see the unusual Pagoda rising up out of the ground and the famous Pym Chair standing to its left. Continuing on your way to the Noe Stool will take you about 15 minutes and those of you feeling energetic enough will no doubt want to climb this small landmark.

Carrying on with the walk you will note to the right a towering crag, Edale Rocks, which is your next port of call. There is no direct path to these rocks, so you will have to make your own route to reach them; bear round them to your right coming up to their summit from the back. From Edale Rocks bear S.W. for the small knoll called the Swine's Back, reached within 15 minutes. Standing on top of its small but flat plateau you can drink in the surrounding moors with excellent views of the Cloughs. The summit is the 6 mile (9 kms.) point of this walk.

Again bearing S.W. you will see a path going down to the medieval cross called Edale Cross; this is your next waymark. From the cross turn right, down towards the Stonyford crossing, cross over the brook but do not cross over the stile. Instead, follow the road down; this is the ancient Over Horse Waie route now called Edale Road. The road passes by Coldwell Clough Farm, then sweeps round until you come to two gates near a bridge fording the River Sett. Take the left-hand gate, walking up the road till you reach the top where there is to be found, on the right-hand side, a large white stone pillar with a hole through the face of it, called the White Lady. Opposite this marker there is a small path going up the banking to a wider path. Follow this up until you reach a wood, Elle Bank. Follow the path through the wood which will bring you out on the fringes of Hayfield Campsite. Follow the course and flow of the River Sett which will bring you into Hayfield.

WALK 2 THE NORTHWEST ARC
Length: 15 miles (24kms.)
Start: Hayfield Finish:Edale
Going: Firm except for two small sections.
Gradient: First section steep, flat, then rising slowly
Time: 7 - 9 hours with time out for viewing, or 6 hours otherwise.

This walk takes in the ruggedness of Kinder whilst the views along the way are exceptional to say the least. It is a fairly long walk starting at Hayfield and ending up at Edale station/car park.

Starting at Hayfield Information Centre, the start of the Sett Valley Trail, cross over the A624 and pass by the church, going over the bridge which spans the Sett and then bear right into Kinder Road. A pleasant walk now confronts you as you amble along through the Kinder Valley. About 1 mile (1½kms.) along the road you will come to the Bowden Bridge quarry where the mass trespass of 1932 took place; note the plaque commemorating this event. Another five minute's walk will bring you to the site of the Kinder Mission, on the banks of the Sett. A little further still and again to your right, over a wall, can be seen the foundations of the old cafe of Mountain View.

The road now drops down to meet the Booth's Bridge which you cross, bearing left on the other side and passing through a gate to come out upon the banks of the Sett. Follow the path till it rises up a grassy banking then turn left over the footbridge fording the Sett. This will bring you out at the entrance to Kinder Reservoir, a private area, but immediately to the left of the entrace can be found a gate which you must pass through. Follow the ensuing path all the way up. At the top Kinder Reservoir opens out before you. Continue following the course of the wall which will bring you out onto White Brow, then proceed onwards till you stand on the shoulder of Nab Brow where the Kinder Amphitheatre opens out before you. Carry on around Nab Brow to the northern catchment of the reservoir; this is the brook that has found its way down from William Clough and which you are now about to climb up. The climb is steady but becomes steeper near the summit. The path is sadly eroded so be very careful.

The summit will be attained when you stand between Mill Hill to your left and the N.W. buttress of Kinder to your right, your next objective. First you have to cross a small section of land that is more often than not rather boggy, but once across, the buttress rises up above you. Do not let the height deceive you, for within twenty minutes or less you will be standing looking down and across at Mill Hill. A well deserved rest is now due for you have covered 5 miles (8kms.) of which a large slice has been climbing - however the climbing is more or less finished. Your walk now continues east along Kinder Edge and if you look closely you should spot fragments of the two crashed Sabres which lie close to the tip of the N.W. buttress. The first well known feature of the Edge lies about 1 mile (1½kms.) from the buttress, the Boxing Glove Stones.

From this point onwards the Edge becomes somewhat rocky and you may come across one or two rock climbers. The views from here and as you walk along are very good; you can even see as far as Yorkshire. The end of this long escarpment is reached at Fairbrook Naze, a very good place to rest and partake in some nourishment whilst you sit and oggle at the views.

Below you flows the Fairbrook and after your rest set off along the Naze until you find a favourable position to drop down and cross over the brook to reach the opposite escarpment of Seal Edge. The first rocky escarpment you encounter will be the summit of the climbers' paradise, the Chinese Wall. Continue onwards noting the Snake Inn down in the valley below until you reach a rocky shoulder. This area is known as the Seal Stones and overlooks Blackden Moor. Follow the path round the shoulder until a brook confronts you, Blackden Brook and once across this brook you stand on one of my favourite spots of Kinder, Blackden Rind. I have spent many an hour here drinking in the tranquility of the surrounding area and the picturesque scenes.

You will now have covered 10 miles (16kms.) - only 5 more to go, but they are 5 miles of scenic splendour once the next small section has been defeated. At Blackden Rind you will find a large flat-topped overhanging rock - climb onto this and turn S.W. looking across and up the peat moor to the horizon where can be seen what appears to be a large rock but which in actual fact is a couple of large boulders; this is Hart's Horn, your next marker. Cross this peat and grough laden moor with care, keeping the Horn in view at all time until it is reached. From here follow the path which leads off in a southerly direction until you stand between Nether and Upper tors, overlooking the picturesque Grindsbrook Valley, and all the surrounding ridges.

Now turn towards the west and follow the path until a huge cleft seems to bar your way. This is the splendid Grindsbrook Towers, best viewed in the spring when the brook flowing between them is in its full cascading glory. Walk the edge of the towers until a safe fording place is found and cross over, turning left on the other side and walking along the other tower until another cleft is met, the head of Grindsbrook Clough. Your route now lies down through this pleasant meandering and scenic clough, but be wary of the descent of the first part for it is extremely rocky. Follow the path all the way through the clough until the boundary of open country sign is reached at Golden Clough. Pass through the gate here and on through the small wood and then across the meadow until the log bridge is reached. Cross over it and then proceed up the other side into Grindsbrook Booth (Edale village) by the side of the Old Nag's Head Inn.

Follow the road past the church and the Fieldhead Information Centre, (if time permits call in the Centre for a browse, it is well worth a visit), five minutes from here and you are at Edale station and the train back to the rat race.

WALK 3 THE SOUTHWEST VALLEYS

Length: 10 miles (16kms.)
Start: Edale Finish: Hayfield
Going: Firm unless very wet weather

Gradient: Moderate excepting Jacob's Ladder
Time: 6 hours with views, 4 hours otherwise.

I particularly like this walk for it is not too strenuous and can be done quite easily in the warm sunny summer evenings. Starting at Edale station/car park walk up the road to the booth of Grindsbrook/Edale village, and at the Old Nag's Head Inn turn to your left and look for the Pennine Way alternative route sign via Upper Booth. Pass through the gate and follow the path marked by arrows and over five stiles that are well spaced out. After the fifth stile you will now be midway round the base of Broadlee Bank Tor. Keep to the path which now veers S.W. taking you down the hillside over two more stiles and passing through two more gates, eventually ending up in the farmyard of Upper Booth. Passing through the farmyard note the unusual siting of the post-box on the stable wall.

Leaving the farmyard via the gate turn right and continue along the broad path passing into Lee Estate. A pleasant walk through the estate will bring you level with the old Lee Farmhouse/cottage which you pass to enter the south-western moors of Kinder. At the 3 mile (5kms.) point you will encounter the old packhorse bridge called Yongate. Under the bridge flows the main tributary of the River Noe which you can see cascading over the rocks as it flows down off the Cloughs, whilst above rises the rocky escarpment of the edge of the Woolpacks and Crowden Tower. As you make your way over the bridge you will note to your left on the hillside the ruins of a farm, which was Edale Head House, the residing place of Jacob Marshall, the innovator of the infamous Jacob's Ladder, which now awaits your pleasure. Ascending the ladder, a long drawn out walk, note the very fine views of the Clough and its many tributaries. Once the ladder has been conquered you will find that the summit a very strategic place to have a rest and take some refreshment, whilst you partake in this you can enjoy the splendid view of the start of the Vale of Edale you have just walked along.

Continuing your journey along the path, which regretfully still rises, you will pass the turn-off via the Swine's Back of the Pennine Way alternative route. This is signposted and the route by the Swine's Back is clearly visible after thousands of people have walked this way. Leaving the signpost behind continue up the hill to the summit where to your right you will locate the medieval cross that was re-erected last century, Edale Cross. The path now drops down to meet with a brook tumbling over many small rocks and stones: Stonyford crossing, the 5 mile point (8kms.). Cross over the brook and over the stile and continue along the narrow path which veers round the base of Kinderlow End. As you come round it you will note that a path veers off from the one you are following; ignore this secondary path but keep to the main one which heads for a corner of a fence and dry stone wall a little way up from the ladder stile. Follow the path from here which runs parallel with the wall, keeping the rising Kinderlow End to your right. A gate confronts you which you pass through, then make for the wall to your left. You will see from this point that the path is channelled down between two stone walls which you will follow until you come to a kissing gate and a signpost for open access. A last lingering view from here of the Three Knolls, Cluther Rocks, Kinder Low and Kinderlow End before you move on and leave it all behind.

After passing through the kissing gate follow the narrow path across the field and through a gap in the wall (where a gate should be) into the next field. Kinder Reservoir comes into view, whilst lying to your right in a small wooded clearing can be seen the very picturesque Upper House. You will not find a better spot to view the whole of this sprawling house. Continue your walk along the path that turns in the direction of the house, to a ladder stile which you climb over and then turn left through a gate onto a very broad stony path heading down to another gate. Pass through this gate and then turn directly to your left, following the path down past Farlands and its lodge until you come to a side road to your left which leads into the cobbled farmyard of Booth. Then proceed through the yard onto a wide dirt road, which is followed on its meandering journey. As you walk along take in a bird's eye view of the upper regions of the Kinder Valley, with splendid views of The Cote and Oak Bank House.

The road eventually enters between the two holdings of Hills House and Hill House Farm, best viewed in the evening as the sun is setting. Continue down the road till you meet up with a bridge crossing the Sett, then turn right, following the road by the side of the Sett until the very old Bowden Bridge comes into view with the River Kinder flowing under it and then being swallowed up by the Sett. Carry on along the road until a sign on a gate tells you that you are entering the Hayfield campsite, pass through the gate or over the adjacent stone stile and continue along the banks of the Sett. The campsite will be left behind as you start a small climb up the road to eventually overlook the cricket pitch of Hayfield. Continue into the village itself and the Information Centre for the bus home.

WALK 4 THE SNAKE AND KINDER DOWNFALL CIRCULAR

Length: 17 miles (27kms.)
Start and Finish: Hayfield
Going: Can be boggy but mostly firm, compass essential
Gradient: Two moderate climbs and one long drawn out climb
Time: 8 - 10 hours average.

This walk is really intended for the long sunny summer days and will really test your fitness. The disadvantage is that once you have arrived at the Snake Inn it is a long walk back, for there is no transport available unless you are prepared to hitch a lift. *This is a warning and must be heeded.* The nearest village or town in any direction from the Snake is about 7 miles (11kms.) away, or another 10 miles (16kms.) to the end of this particular walk.

Start the walk from the Hayfield Information Centre as in Walk 2 onto Kinder road, and follow the road until the top of the hill is reached. Look out now for a large wall to your left where a signpost stands above signalling the start of the Snake Path. A meandering climb follows the path up and across a field and through several kissing gates until the land levels out. From this point a short walk will bring you to a large gate, access to the barren Middle Moor. Pass through the gate and follow the well-defined path, your objective is the white shooting cabin in the distance. Near the cabin a signpost will confront you. At this point bear slightly right, bye-passing the cabin completely. This will bring you out above White Brow, commanding a very good view of the Kinder Reservoir. Follow the path round which drops down to the northern end of Nab Brow and the base of William Clough. A climb is now imminent up this clough - so up you go, and on attaining the top you will have covered 4 miles (6½kms.), most of it on firm ground. Now prepare yourself for a bit of bogtrotting!

Your route lies straight on and round Ashop Head, a most inhospitable place, where if you are not careful you can end up to your thighs in the thick squelchy peat. This terrain takes about fifteen minutes, then the going underfoot gets a little easier though a few more boggy stretches do confront you, but the scenery of the Ashop Valley offsets this minor inconvenience. After about 6 miles (9kms.) a badly delapidated shooting cabin will come into view whilst just past it the path passes over the base of Upper Gate Clough and then Nether Gate Clough. From here on you enter a different world, where the terrain becomes firmer and flat. To your left the River Ashop cascades

Punch's Nose, a severe climb on Ashop Edge, the north edge of Kinder. Ashop Clough in the background.

through a mini gorge before it enters the heavily wooded area of the Woodlands Valley.

A magnificent sight awaits you, for after entering the massif Snake Plantation you take but a short walk through it until you exit out into an impressive picturesque valley, best viewed on a sunny day. The valley has everything - a river cascading over rocks creating mini waterfalls, towering conifers, pleasant lush grass which is dotted here and there with rocks and to finish it off, a log bridge. Amble through at your own pleasure, finally crossing the log bridge to an exit on the Snake Pass road, a little way up from the Snake Inn. This is your first big resting point; rest well because your next section is a long hard climb, your last climb of the walk.

Carry on down the road for a very short distance till you come to an access point on your right into the forest. Follow the path down to the River Ashop locating the footbridge and then crossing over. To your left will be the end of the Fair Brook, which you climb up. It is an extremely long meandering walk to the summit on the edge of the Plateau, but again the scenery outweighs all the bad points of this stiff climb. If you walk steadily and admire the views then in no time at all you will be at the top and will have covered 10 miles (16kms.).

The order of the day is now compass work, for you have to cross the Plateau from this point to Kinder Downfall. The direction you require is directly west from the summit of the Fair Brook. It is inadvisable to cross the Plateau if the weather is misty, instead, divert around Fairbrook Naze and then along The Edge to the N.W. buttress and drop down into William Clough. When crossing the Plateau keep to the bearing and look for a V-shape on the horizon, which indicates the Kinder Downfall summit. It should only take about 15 to 20 minutes providing you tread warily over the peat and the groughs.

On reaching the Downfall your second long rest is due. In all probability you will not be alone here, for there is nearly always somebody here at any time of the day providing the weather is fine.

The last lap now awaits you and it is all downhill from here. Head south along the path which overlooks the valley below, until you come upon a large fissure, Red Brook, which if it is summer time will more than likely be dry. Cross over the fissure at its summit and follow the path that starts to descend. This will lead you into the Cluther Rocks and then onto the Three Knolls. Once over the knolls you will find yourself at the base of Kinderlow End where a gate is to be found. Pass through, continuing the downward trend until a ladder stile is spotted on your right-hand side. Over the stile and you find yourself on Harry Moor. Follow the path over this small moor, through a kissing gate then over farmland to another kissing gate. Cross more farmland then over another stile, dropping down into Tunstead Clough Farm. Follow the path around the farm and continue till you exit at the road and bridge over the River Sett. Turn right here, following the road to Bowden Bridge and continuing on from here as in the end of Walk 3, finally reaching Hayfield and the bus home for tea.

WALK 5 THE SOUTHERN PLANE CRASH SITES CIRCULAR

Length: 10 miles (16kms.)
Start and Finish: Edale
Going: Can be boggy at times and not advisable in misty weather
Gradient: Very Moderate
Time: 5 - 6 hours very steady.

A walk that is not very tiring and can if need be spread out to take in the biggest part of the day just admiring the splendid views.

Edale is where you start. From the station/car park follow the road up to Grindsbrook Booth (Edale village), pass by the Old Nag's Head Inn, locating the Pennine Way sign. Cross over the log bridge fording the Grinds Brook and continue along the path on the opposite side. Follow the path that keeps the Grinds Brook company all the way through the valley of Grindsbrook Clough. As you amble along note the very fine views of The Nab, Ringing Roger, Nether Tor, Upper Tor and Far Upper Tor whilst to your left lies the rock strewn area of the Fox Holes overshadowed by Grindslow Knoll. Near the head of the clough you will be confronted by two large clefts, in front of you the very rocky head of the clough, to your right the cleft is bounded by the high Grindsbrook Towers. You will take the former and though it looks quite steep you will be surprised to find yourself standing on the top looking down along the valley you have just walked through within 15 minutes. Turn now in the direction of the Grindsbrook Towers and proceed along the left-hand edge until the brook or dry bed, depending on the weather and time of year, is reached. A most pleasant and lonely walk along this brook/bed confronts you as it meaders along its merry way off the Plateau.

Your first landmark will lie on the left-hand bank, the ruins of the Four Jacks Cabin. Pass on by the ruins until the brook/bed forks left and right, take the left-hand fork climbing out from the brook/bed onto the Plateau itself. Follow the course of the bed, but look out for a small level area that has flat slabs of rock and gritstone sand, where a small search will locate the wreckage of an Anson. After your inspection turn about face in the direction you have just come, look across the Plateau and you will see a small rise in the terrain culminating in a small knoll, this is Wove Hill your next point of call. A short walk will find you standing at its base. Scout around the south side of its base and you will locate a pile of fragments and pieces of a Dragon Rapide. At this point, 4 miles (6½kms.), I would suggest you have a little rest upon the hill's summit, whilst you take in the barren, but surprisingly pleasant surroundings.

Afterwards, retrace your steps to the Grindsbrook Towers and find a place to cross over to the opposite tower. Once across turn right, making for the escarpment overlooking the Grindsbrook Valley. Your first escarpment will be the Far Upper Tor where you have to look carefully to locate some small fragments of a Wellington Bomber. Sometimes somebody takes the trouble of collecting the fragments together and placing them in a small pile on the summit of the tor. You may be lucky and time will be saved in locating the fragments, but if it has been windy they will have been scattered again. Continuing onwards, keep to the edge, admiring the great views of the valley below and the surrounding terrain, passing Upper and Nether Tor. Once you have passed Nether Tor you will come to the summit of Golden Clough; cross over and then bear N.E., heading out onto the Plateau again. As you walk up the sodden peat terrain, the O.S. pillar of Blackden Edge will come into view. This is your 7 mile (11kms.) point.

From the pillar walk directly north for a few paces where you will locate fragments of a Halifax bomber. Return to the pillar then bear off in a south-easterly direction for about a hundred paces. On this line will be found a pile of wreckage, this is the remains of another Wellington bomber.

The crash sites now complete; you turn your attention to the journey back to Edale. This is easier than you might think. Leave the Wellington remains and head due south over the small stretch of peat, coming out on the escarpment overlook the Vale of Edale. Your position will be somewhere between the crags of the Rowland Cote Moor edge to your left and the Ringing Roger to your right. Roughly in front of you and bearing downwards will be the long but straight clough of the Oller Brook, your route back to Edale.

Drop down into the clough locating the path as you do so and following it all the way to the small booth of Ollerbrook, passing as you do Lands Barn near the booth. From Ollerbrook you have a choice of two paths back into Edale, you can either bear to your right following the paths which exit out at either the Fieldhead Centre or into Grindsbrook Booth, or instead carry on with the path you are on which will drop down to the main thoroughfare, Hope road. Both routes are about the same length and whichever you chose, Edale station/car park only lies about 1 mile (1½kms.) from Ollerbrook Booth.

WALK 6 THE SOUTHWEST RIDGE CIRCUIT

Length: 14 miles (23kms.)
Start and Finish: Edale
Going: Some bog trotting and a compass essential
Not advisable in mist
Gradient: Very Moderate
Time: 7 - 9 hours including viewing or 6 hours otherwise.

An excellent walk for those who like the high ground and love to see the valleys below. The most strenuous climb is at the beginning but this is nothing compared with a lot of the walks.

You start by following Walk 5 to the summit and head of Grindsbrook Clough, from where you pick up the path that heads westwards, the Pennine Way route. Keep to this path until it meets up with another path coming in at a tangent from Grindslow Knoll. These paths converge and then split again, one going slightly left the other right (which in actual fact is the Pennine Way). You take the left-hand path for the time being - you will meet up with the other later. Follow the path till you cross the summit of Crowden Brook, lying in the shadow of the towering Crowden Tower; amble up to the top of the tower to take advantage of the excellent views of the valley and moors below.

Retrace your steps down to the summit of Crowden Brook then follow it up and out onto the wild Kinder Plateau. When you start to lose the main brook take a bearing with your compass, setting it to N.N.W. (around the 340° mark) and then proceed along this course. You will pass (probably without knowing it) the second highest point on Kinder, Crowden Head. It is about this point where the butterflies in your stomach begin to flutter. The Kinder Plateau is a barren land of peat and open sky - when you attempt walks such as this one onto the plateau it can be quite an experience. Do not despair, for you are on the main Pennine Way route and though there is no recognised path to follow just trust your compass. Eventually after a good mile (1½kms.) of navigating the peat hags you will come across the wide bed of the Kinder River, here at its infancy. Turn right onto the bed following the flow of the river till you come to two large prominent rocks on either side of the river: Kinder Gates, your passport onto the last stretch before the magnificent Kinder Downfall. From this point it is but a short walk round the river's bend to the Downfall, the 6 mile (9kms.) point and a well deserved rest.

Strength renewed, you now set off on the long arc back to Edale, taking the path southwards along the edges, keeping the valley below to your right. Keep to the paths on the upward trend and do not take any paths that appear to go down the hillside. As you ramble along you will perceive some splendid views of the land westwards, more so on a very bright and clear day. Your route will take you over the top of Red Brook, then onwards passing a number of small rock outcrops. The next main landmark you will encounter will be the Kinder Low Ordnance Survey pillar and its companion, the large stone cairn. Pass by the cairn, locating a path that is easily discernible, down to the

Edale Rocks, a large rock that can be seen in the distance, seemingly at the end of the path.

Reaching the Edale Rocks, skirt around the base, bearing to your right and coming round to the front. Heading down the hill to the dry stone wall at the bottom. This reached you will see the wide alternative Pennine Way route coming up the hill, so make your way round to it and then proceed down to a signpost (irrelevant to this walk). Three options are now open to you; you can either carry on with this walk for another 6 miles (9kms.) or divert to your left, following the path down Jacob's Ladder then on through the Lee Estate and the Vale of Edale via Upper Booth and Barber Booth and back to the station at Edale, 4 miles (6½kms.) from this point. Or alternatively, you could turn to your right, follow the path up to Edale Cross and then on down to the Stonyford crossing, passing into Coldwell Clough and subsequently into Hayfield, again 4 miles away.

If you choose to carry on with the walk, continue in a straight line up the opposite hillside till you reach the top and it levels out. Follow the path that starts to bear S.E. Into view will appear the O.S. pillar of Brown Knoll, your next objective. You will first have to cross the Brown Knoll Ditch which can be quite tricky, especially if there has been a fair amount of rain recently. Once across make for the pillar. You are now out of open access land, though the landowners kindly allow you to pass through; at certain points you will pass in and out of National Trust land. From the O.S. pillar proceed along the path that bears S.E. onto the fringes of Horsehill Tor passing as you do so an old boundary stone.

The path now drops slightly coming around to meet the Great Ridge. Follow the path round the summit of the hill, passing over a clough called Whitemoor where you will have an excellent view of the head of the Vale of Edale. Keep to the path around the top of the hill till you meet up with a signpost indicating the Chapel Gate Tract. This is the main path back into Edale, but you require the small faint path that runs north down the hill from the signpost. This path will bring you to the bottom of Whitemoor Clough, pass over two stiles and head for the small centre of Dalehead where you will have 2 more miles (3kms.) left to walk.

Continue on the road out of Dalehead, noting as you do so to your left and right some small grassy mounds; The Tips, slag and wastage heaps from the construction of the Cowburn Tunnel. The path continues through grazing land, eventually leading onto the road. If you turn right this brings you into Barber Booth, where there is a shop, if you require some form of nourishment. Continue along the road, passing the Waterside camping and caravan site, until back at the station/car park.

WALK 7 THE KINDER AMPHITHEATRE WALK

Length: 12 miles (20kms.)
Start and Finish: Hayfield
Going: Usually very firm but stony and rocky
Gradient: Moderate to steep
Time: 6 - 7 hours.

A pleasant walk, though not as scenic as most, this is best attempted in the winter when there is very little snow but there have been some very keen frosts, cold enough to freeze water. The frozen Downfall is a magnificent sight.

From the Hayfield Information Centre make your way onto the Hayfield - Glossop road, A624, then proceed up the road in the direction of Glossop. Carry on along the road and down the hill, where, on the right-hand side of the road will be found the entrance and drive to Park Hall. Make you way to the end of the drive where it bends to the left and subsequently Park Hall.

Instead of following the road around the bend (unless of course you want a quick view of the hall) make for the large gate in front of you. Pass through the gate which will bring you out onto the Middle Moor. This rises up before you, so follow the path up onto the moor where it will marry up with the Snake Path.

The signpost before the white shooting cabin is your destination. Once this is reached bear off to your right, locating a very faint path that comes in at a tangent from the one you have just walked along over Middle Moor. Keep to this path until it reaches a gap in a dry-stone wall. Go through the gap, then abruptly turn right (Beware! If you do not turn right you will end up in the quarry below). As you turn right you will notice a wire fence in front of you. There is a stile at the end of the fence which you climb over; you have now entered the dead world of the Oldpits Plantation. Turn to your left and walk to the rocky edge, the Heron Rock, one of my favourite spots. Stay awhile here and take in the magical beauty of the Kinder Amphitheatre and the farmlands of Farlands and Booth.

Retrace your steps back to the signpost near the shooting cabin and then continue along the path that overlooks the reservoir. Follow this down over Nab Brow till you stand at the foot of William Clough. You are not going up the clough on this walk. Instead, cross over the brook's feeder to the reservoir and turn to your right, taking the path up the northern end of the reservoir. Cross over the stile then turn to your right again, following the fence down to the reservoir wall. Follow this wall all the way round until you meet up with the reservoir feeder of the River Kinder. Follow the river upwards, the right-hand bank is more favourable, until you are confronted by a wire fence where you will find two stiles, one on each bank of the river. Climb over - you will find a small spinney, Peter Nook Wood, lying on the left-hand side of the river.

Continue up the river again, the right-hand bank is still the more favourable side, and as you start to leave the wood behind so the river starts to cascade. A wooden fence and stile will appear before long, and at this point there are two mini waterfalls and two large pools. This is The Runge, usually frozen in the winter but very inviting on a hot sunny summer's day. Once over this part the terrain starts to level out, but not for long for the ground starts to rise steeply, becoming rockier the higher you climb until you round the Kinder Buttress. Now the way up is very steep and very rocky. If this walk is attempted in the snow laden months of winter, your task from this point is trebled, for the snow tends to drift and cover the rocks making the walk extremely difficult. However, assuming there is very little snow then it is not too bad, though it seems quite demanding at times. Your objective will now be in plain view, the magnificent Kinder Downfall, frozen in all its glory. As you near the foot of the falls the terrain now becomes very hard to scramble over, but with a bit of huffing and puffing you should manage it and stand in awe at this magnificent sight. (If you do this walk in summer, you will want to stand behind the actual waterfall; this is quite possible without even getting wet.) You have now covered 6 miles (9kms.) the last 2 miles being the most arduous.

Retrace your steps down the river until the Red Brook, a tributary of the River Kinder, is met at its confluence with the river. Cross over the river at this point, scrambling up the opposite hill until it levels out at the top. A short walk along this mini plateau will bring you to the legendary Mermaid's Pool, but unless it is Easter Sunday you will not see the mermaid. From the pool walk westwards to the edge of the plateau and look down, locating Peter Nook Wood. Take your time and go with care on your way down into the wood, for the hillside here can be quite tricky. Pass through the wood, making your way down to the River Kinder, whereupon you retrace your steps back to the foot of William Clough. From this point you have 3 miles (5kms.) left to walk, so recross the brook taking the path onto Nab Brow and follow the lower path all the way round the reservoir onto White Brow. Keep the reservoir wall to your left and drop down a stony path and pass through the gate at the bottom. This will bring you out at the Kinder Reservoir entrance. You cross the footbridge to be found here then turn right, following the course of the River Kinder, and pass through another gate, then on and over Booth Bridge. Kinder road now lies before you through the splendid Kinder Valley where at the end lies Hayfield and transport home.

WALK 8 THE KINDER DOWNFALL CIRCULAR

Length: 12 miles (20kms.)
Start and Finish: Hayfield
Going: Soft to firm
Gradient: Moderate
Time: About 5 hours.

This pleasant walk takes in several sections of walks previously mentioned, so if you are walking them in order you should now be familiar with the relevant sections.

Starting once again from the Hayfield Information Centre make your way along the Kinder Valley as in the start of Walk 2, as far as Booth Bridge. Cross the bridge and follow the road up past Farlands until you come to a sort of T-junction. This next section you will have covered in the middle-end section of Walk 3, only now you will be walking it in reverse. At the T-junction turn to your right and pass through the gate following the road up the hill till you reach a fence, then bear right again and climb over the ladder stile. Proceed along the path which bears left after a short walk and follow the path across the grazing land. Once again a splendid view of Upper House may be obtained as you make your way over this land, whilst in the distance lies Kinder Low. Pass through a dry-stone wall, continuing over the farmland to the other dry-stone wall looming up in the distance. At the wall you will meet a kissing gate; go on through and turn to your right, walking up between two dry-stone walls. Keep between these until the left-hand wall ends. At this point turn left, heading in the direction of the rising Kinderlow End. As you reach its base you will cross onto a path. Turn to your left on reaching this path and follow it as it meanders up and over the Three Knolls. Leaving these behind you will now enter a very rocky area, the Cluther Rocks, the 5 mile point (8kms.). Take time out here to locate the old abandoned mill stones which can be found just below the Cluther Rocks. Continuing your walk follow the path which now starts to rise, eventually coming out at the Red Brook. Cross on over to the other side where you will be standing on the fringes of the plateau with the valley falling away below you. Proceed onwards along this edge until the Kinder Downfall is attained. You will have covered exactly half of this walk at this point.

Fit and eager to be on your way again, cross the river, attaining the opposite bank above the Downfall and locate the path heading out north. A pleasant and scenic walk along the edges ensures that you will not become bored, for the terrain along here varies considerably. You will find yourself walking between large rocks, over flat slabs of rocks, across small peat sections, over the rocky Sandy Heys and passing over the summit of Upper Western Buttress, whilst at the same time taking in the splendid view of the valley and countryside below.

The last rocks you will encounter on the edges of this walk will be the upper region of the Mill Hill Rocks, and a short walk from here will bring you to the N.W. buttress of Kinder with Mill Hill lying opposite and in between the path connecting them. Descend down the buttress onto the path until you stand between both the hills, then turn towards the Kinder Reservoir and make your way down William Clough. Take care for the path through this clough is subject to erosion in places. At the foot of the clough pass onto Nab Brow and make your way back into Hayfield as in the end section of Walk 7.

WALK 9 THE ANCIENT PATHS CIRCUIT

Length: 10 miles (16kms.)
Start and Finish: Hayfield
Going: Usually very firm
Gradient: Very, very moderate
Time: 4 - 5 hours is about average for this walk.

This walk is ideal for a family well equipped with walking boots, because it does not stray far from Hayfield and is on a par with a jaunt round your local woods. It keeps to recognised footpaths, but one section can be quite wet and boggy after heavy rain though not deep - meaning it will not cover your boots!

Once again we start at the Information Centre at Hayfield. Make for the subway under the A624, passing under and coming out in the village of Hayfield near the George public house. Turn to your right, going up the hill till the road forks at the top, when you take the right-hand fork, Highgate road. Highgate is long and moderately steep. After about 1 mile (1½kms.) you will find that this road also forks. Take the left-hand fork this time onto the dirt track between two dry-stone walls.

Walking along this section you will be walking where the Romans once marched, for this road was known to be used by them in the time of their conquest. This section of the road is quite long and straight with a slight rise in the gradient. At the top of the road a gate will need to be opened for you to pass on through. Once through here you will find that the path continues around the base of the hill lying to your left, which is the western flank of Mount Famine. Proceed along the path curving around the hill till another gate confronts you, where you will enter into the area of open access and Kinder will start to open out before you.

First of all it is worth making a couple of minor climbs to take in some splendid scenery. On entering the open access area bear off to your left, locating and climbing up the path that will bring you out onto the summit of Mount Famine - at the most it will only take you about ten minutes. At the summit turn in a full circle, taking in some of the most beautiful and often rugged terrain hereabouts - though the best is yet to come.

Retrace your steps down Mount Famine till you once again stand on the path at the boundary of open access, then make your way along the path to two stone gate pillars. From this point on it is locally known as the Dimpus Gate Track. The track originated some three hundred years ago and connected Hayfield with Castleton via Rushup Edge. As you walk between the pillars a small pyramid-shaped hill will rise up on your right-hand side; this is South Head. Continue around the base of it ignoring the signpost in front. A few paces beyond the signpost the path will have reached its apex and appears to drop into the valley below; this is as far as you will be walking on this particular path. On the left is a dry-stone wall that wanders off across the moor. Bear this in mind but for the time being turn to your right. Above you rises South Head and a faint path can be just made out on its journey to the top. It looks fairly steep but within ten minutes you will have attained the small cairn of stones that tops the pinnacle. If you thought the views from Mount Famine were excellent then from South Head you will be doubly pleased. This is an ideal spot to have a short rest whilst you take in the sweeping views of all the valleys below you and the ridges and moors above them. At this point you will have covered a very steady 3 miles (5kms.).

Retrace your steps down the hillside till you stand facing the wall that disappears into the horizon across the moor, which in fact is called Dimpus. The wall is your guide across the moor, as at certain points the faint path often disappears. Keep the wall to your right as you attempt to walk across the moor and do not stray more than a few paces from it. After a good walk you will be confronted by a fence strung across the moor, crossed by a stile. Not far from the stile the wall does a sharp right turn and then turns left again further on, but you can cut off the angle to meet up with it once again some fifty paces further on. The moor now starts to rise and over to your left rises the Swine's Back, and it is around this point that you will actually see the best view of the Swine's Back. The wall to your right will now disappear only to be replaced by a wire fence, erected to keep the moorland sheep from destroying any more vegetation. As you reach the top of the moor use one of the stiles that are provided for you to cross the fence, and on the other side will be found a well defined path; follow this path down the hill, keeping the wire fence to your left this time.

At the bottom of the hill you will find a signpost denoting the alternative Pennine Way, but your route does not lie this way. Instead, turn west (to your left) and proceed up the hill till you encounter the medieval boundary marker of Edale Cross. This is an ideal time and place to take your last rest before attempting the last 4 miles (6½kms.).

From the Cross drop down the path to meet up with the brook at Stonyford crossing, cross over the brook and continue down the main path, Edale road, formerly Over Horse Waie. This was the old packhorse route connecting Hayfield to Edale and the towns and villages beyond. Carry on straight down the hill till you come upon Coldwell Clough cottage/farm on your right-hand side. Look carefully at the roof of the barn that can be seen just behind the cottage, and you should be able to see a stone monkey perched on the end.

From the farm trace the road round until you come upon two gates near a bridge fording the Sett, as in Walk 1. This time take the right-hand gate, proceeding through the small valley, near the end of which you will notice to your right Ashes Farm. The road in front of you now starts to rise, but it is only a minor hill. From the top of the rise continue downwards and cross over the bridge at the bottom. You will now be in familiar territory, for from this point onwards follow the route as described at the end of Walk 3.

WALK 10 THE NORTHWESTERN MOORS CIRCULAR

Length: 12 miles (20kms.)
Start and Finish: Glossop
Going: Plenty of bog trotting. Compass essential; the area is prone to mist
Gradient: Very moderate
Time: About 6 hours is the average.

A demanding walk only recommended for the hardy walker. Though there is very little gradient climbing it is the moors that sap your energy.

This walk starts at the Norfolk Arms, Glossop town centre. Cross over the main road and proceed up the A624, Hayfield, Chapel en le Frith road. After about 1½ miles (2kms.) you will come across a small slip road bearing off from the A624. A sign will point to Moorfield. Walk down this slip road where at the bottom you will note a ladder stile, climb up and over it and proceed up either of the two paths in front of you. The paths lead up the hill where in the distance to your right you will note another ladder stile; this is your next objective. Upon reaching the stile climb over and proceed up the path, which will take you onto a number of rocks that meander slightly, hence the name Worm Stones. Below these stones lies the long and bleached summit of Whitehorn Clough with a shooting cabin standing on the flanks of the clough. Continue on your way across Shaw Moor. You will note as you go higher the flora becomes more colourful, but this will change shortly to the more drab looking vegetation of heathland scrub. At the top of the hill an O.S. pillar will appear. This is Harry Hut and once reached it is advisable to have a decent rest, for in front of you lies the morass of Leygatehead Moor.

There is no recognised path from this point for quite a bit - but not to worry, face E.S.E. where you will perceive in the far distance the N.W. buttress of Kinder. Follow through on this bearing, crossing the tangled undergrowth of this barren moor, until you meet up with the main path across the moor. This should take you about fifteen minutes from the O.S. pillar of Harry Hut.

The main path having been reached, follow it over the moor in the general direction of Kinder. Some way along the path and lying to the left of it will be found an almost complete wing and various other remains of a crashed Liberator Bomber, scattered along a shallow gully with further remains found a little bit further on lying on a flat bare patch of land. Leaving the Libertor behind it is just a short walk to the summit of Mill Hill, where you will have covered 4 miles (6½kms.).

Rest here and take in the magnificent view of the N.W. buttress of the Kinder massif before you attempt the next section, part of the Pennine Way. This will be a strong test of stamina if there has been much recent rain - it will also be a bog squelching experience. Providing there is no mist (and the area is renowned for it) then there is not much trouble in following the course of this well-trodden path, which becomes increasingly boggy every year. Keeping as near to it as possible and for safety set your compass, taking a bearing off your map between Mill Hill and Glead Hill, your next objective, for as previously mentioned, mists do appear suddenly in this region. Your bearing will be N.E. - about 45°. Following the course of the path, finding as you go along that this section is waymarked by several stakes embedded in the peat. The path will rise slightly and eventually you will stand on a small ridge overlooking a dip in the terrain. On the opposite knoll can be seen a thick wooden post - this is Glead Hill -whilst away to your left in the distance you should be able to make out the Snake Pass summit. Upon reaching the summit of Glead Hill you will find it advisable not to go near the post for it tends to be rather deep bog here.

From now on the going to the Snake Pass summit is tougher; a lot of minor detours are necessary around the path as it becomes a sea of peat hags and bogs. Another bearing from Glead Hill to the Snake Pass summit is necessary if the weather looks doubtful, otherwise your objective will be in view most of the time. Your bearing now is much the same as the previous one although you will at first veer slightly to your right, coming back in again not far from the pass. If by some chance a mist does suddenly enshroud you catching you unprepared and you feel completely disorientated, do not panic - set your compass for directly north and proceed, taking extreme care as you do so. At the most, thirty minutes will see you standing on the edge of the Snake road at some point.

The Snake Pass summit having been reached you will be glad of a rest and you can breath a sigh of relief after crossing that sea of peat. In front of your rises the southern fringes of the forbidding Bleaklow, a land mass of deep groughs and oceans of peat and very little else -but that is another story. From here you have 5 miles (8kms.) left and a choice of three routes back into Glossop. Firstly, you can encroach onto the first section of the Bleaklow massif and follow the old Roman route called Doctor's Gate down through the Shelf Valley; a very pleasant walk with fine views of the more southerly escarpments of Bleaklow. Secondly, you can follow the meandering Snake road down into the town centre, taking in as you do so some excellent views of the surrounding moors. However, to complete this walk you will be following the third option, keeping to the outer fringes of Kinder and walking along one of my favourite cloughs, Holden Clough.

Proceed down the Snake road in the direction of Glossop, and after about 1 mile (1½kms.) you will see on your left-hand side a narrow gully. Drop into this, for this is the head of Holden Clough, and from here it is all downhill - though it is not all plain sailing! The upper regions of this clough are extremely rocky and you will find yourself criss-crossing the brook on several occasions, trying to find a favourable route down. The brook glints and gleams if the sun is shining as it cascades over the numerous rocks. On your way down you will come upon numerous wrecks of cars that have swerved off the Snake road which towers above you, and also for some inexplicable reason, a number of tin drums pock-mark the way. Halfway down the clough opens out into a large basin; one of my favourite haunts, especially so in the spring, for here a lot of sheep seem to congregate to bear offspring. It is a most enjoyable sight to see the lambs basking in this secluded little basin.

Leaving this area behind, the going gets a little easier, though often you will find yourself walking at an angle on the flanks of the clough. Generally, you will now keep to the right-hand bank. Trees and shrubs start to appear, bringing in more colour. Eventually you will come upon the cascading waterfall of Ramsley Clough as it meets up with the brook from Holden Clough, and from this point onwards the brook becomes Hurst Brook. Follow the brook till it reaches Hurst Reservoir, pass through a gate that lies to the right of the brook and proceed up the path that skirts the reservoir. This drops down into the front of the reservoir then skirts around Glossop golf course. Pass on by the club house, and where the path meets the road turn right. A few paces will bring you out onto the main road into Glossop town centre and the bus or train home.

WALK 11 THE OLD LEGENDS WALK

Length: 10 miles (16kms.)
Start: Bamford Finish: Edale
Going: Very firm
Gradient: Extremely steep
Time: 6 - 8 hours.

This walk embraces fact, fiction, folklore and legend. It can also be quite demanding on stamina, so you have been warned! The walk starts at Bamford station and ends at Edale station, but in between you will take in some of the best scenic view of the Dark Peak, with something to appeal to everybody.

Before you reach the start of the Kinder massif at Yorkshire Bridge you have a forty minute walk. From Bamford station turn right, following the road towards the church and through the quiet and charming village of Bamford and to the semi-country road beyond. To your right will be seen the towering crags of Bamford Edge whilst to your left rises the pinnacle of Win Hill. A row of terraced houses will come into view on the left-hand side of the road, and immediately before these you will see a signpost bearing the direction of Thornhill, which points down a steep road. At the bottom you will cross the double-arched Yorkshire Bridge. Prepare yourself for a back sweating climb up the Yorkshire Bridge Track via Parkin Clough. However, alternately you could take the longer route round by the Ladybower Dam and then up onto the Thornhill Carr Track, cutting back onto the upper regions of Parkin Clough.

For the Yorkshire Bridge Track turn right, pass through a gate then immediately turn to your left where you will see the makings of a path and steps cut out of the earth. Once you are on the path you must stick with it: the main path is crossed several times by minor paths which you must ignore completely. Though it does not seem so nowadays this track is a former packhorse route, of some antiquity. The top of the path is reached when you climb over a stile. From here bear slightly to your right, locating a path that proceeds up the hill in front of you, through the fringes of the Winhill Plantation. Midway up the hill you will have to cross over a ladder stile, then on again till you attain the summit and Ordnance Survey pillar of the dominating peak of Win Hill.

You will now have covered 2½ miles (4kms.), the last mile being a backsweating slog. You will now find it all worthwhile. Time now to unload your rucksack from your back for a while, whilst you take in the spectacular views from this point; Ladybower and its prominent architectural arches set amongst the crags and the moors of the High Peak. Whilst taking all this in think about the old legend of the great Northumbrian army that was once encamped on this hill. I bet they did not march up here via Parkin Clough otherwise they would have been too tired to do battle!

Your next stage lies over the Thornhill Brink, the Hope Brink and onto Hope Cross. Stand at the O.S. pillar and look westwards where these paths are clearly outlined against the barren moor. Descend from the Pike onto the first path, Thornhill Brink, proceed along the path admiring the splendid views as you do so. If you look carefully you should just be able to see the top of Wooler Knoll peeping out from above the tall conifer trees away to your right. As you draw level with the knoll, which has now become obscured, look over to your left into the valley below where can be seen the small community of Edale End. At about this point you will arrive on the Hope Brink, an old Roman route. Continue along this ridge ignoring all the other minor paths leading onto or off it. Away to your left over the valley can be seen Jaggers' Clough with the Nether Moor quarry lying on its left-hand flank; this is where you are heading so take this opportunity to look at the opposite terrain as you go along the brink.

About forty minutes out from Win Hill, Hope Cross will confront you. The Cross is a very old landmark but is topped by a modern plinth bearing the names of Glossop, Edale, Hope and Sheffield. Pass through the gate behind, continuing on the main path until you reach a signpost and stile close to Crookstone Barn. Cross the stile and take the path that is signposted for Clough Farm; this path runs parallel for a while to the path you have just come along on the opposite side of the valley. The path eventually drops down into Jaggers' Clough; a former packhorse route, some three hundred years old. Ford the brook at the bottom and note as you do so the pleasant little valley here as it meanders upwards. Pass through the gate on the other side and make your way round the erosion barriers, then bear to your left, going up the hillside till you reach the summit of this small hill, lying below Nether Moor. To your right there is the remains of a dry-stone wall which leads up and onto Nether Moor, bypassing the nearby quarry. This is your next stage, but first, after covering 6 miles (9kms.) I strongly advise a good rest before attempting this next section, for it is no picnic and anyway, the views are not too bad from here.

Strong and stout of heart again, set off following the wall up onto the moor. The going underfoot is very rough and there is no footpath so you will be crossing the tangled moorland heather. If it is summer the way ahead is covered with tall green ferns adding a bit more hindrance to your journey. When the dry-stone wall comes to an end, carry on along the same course, looking as you do for a small knoll lying on the summit of the moor's edge. Once located, make your way over to it; this is the site of an ancient Druids' altar and was the former site of an O.S. pillar. The knoll is easily picked out when you arrive on the flat top of the moor, for the ground around is littered with the remains of the cairn.

From here cross the small plateau, heading straight for the hill of Upper Moor, which rises in front of you. The remains of a dry-stone wall will once again cross your path with another directly behind; pass through here and up the hill in front till a path is reached on its upper regions. Ignore this path and continue upwards for a few more paces where you will come upon another path. Turn left onto this and it will bring you round to the Druids' Stone, reputedly used by the Druids, though not for sacrifices as is commonly imagined. The views from here are exceptional, taking in with a sweeping arc the Great Ridge, the Vale of Edale, Winnat's Pass, The Blue John Mine, The Hope Valley, Ladybower Reservoir and the Ashopton Viaduct. A very opportune place for the Druids to hold counsel!

You will now have covered only 7½ miles (12kms.) but it will feel a lot more than that; however, there is not far to go now.

Continue along the path from the Druids' Stone, the path descending slightly onto the escarpment overlooking the Rowland Cote Moor. Pass over a badly depleted stone wall, walking on for a short while until you are confronted with a cleft running down into Edale. This is Ollerbrook Clough, so locate the path running through the clough and proceed down into Edale using the route described at the end of Walk 5.

WALK 12 THE WOODLANDS VALLEY CIRCULAR

Length: 13 miles (21½kms.)
Start and Finish: Edale
Going: Fairly firm
Gradient: Moderate to steep
Time: 8 hours very steady or 6 hours otherwise.

A picturesque walk that takes in a large part of Walk 2, so you may be familiar with the terrain.

Once again you start at Edale, only this time follow the main thoroughfare of the vale, Hope road. You proceed in the direction of Hope, passing over Yemen's Bridge noting the very fine views of the surrounding hills and vale as you meander along. To your left you have the southern edges of Kinder whilst away to your right there is Mam Tor, Back Tor and Lose Hill - the Great Ridge. On the horizon lies the ancient Hope Brink path which in turn is overshadowed by the tall conifers of the Woodlands Valley/Ladybower Plantations. The road continues onwards passing a row of terraced houses, where there is also a small shop. This small community comes under the small booth of Ollerbrook, even though the hamlet is some way off over the fields. Lying at the end of this row of houses and set just behind, can be found the now defunct Edale mill.

Follow the road round and under the railway bridge then on and through Nether Booth, often called Lady Booth.

Once through the booth the road again straightens out. You must look for an old signpost pointing the way to the now submerged hamlets of Derwent Woodlands and Ashopton. This signpost will be on your left and set back from the road slightly.

Follow the directions of the signpost, passing through a small gate onto a narrow bridle road which is quite often boggy after a period of rain. The path rises slowly and skirts around the back of Clough Farm. Cross over the small brook and pass through the gate to gain access to the meadowland beyond. The path now starts to rise up the hill lying below Nether Moor, eventually coming out to overlook Jaggers' Clough, the 3 mile (5kms.) point.

This next section is part of Walk 11 but done in reverse. Drop down into Jaggers' Clough, ford the brook and amble up the path on the hill facing you till you reach the signpost at the top. From the signpost bear directly left; providing the signpost has not been moved in any way, it will point to Alport Bridge.

Follow the path up the hill, passing close by Crookstone Barn. Go up and through a gate, then bear to your left, but first look back at the splendid view of the western catchment area of the Ladybower Reservoir. As you turn left you will come over the top of Crookstone Hill and drop down onto the path that crosses the summit of Blackley Clough. Continue on a N.W. course along Blackley Hey in the Woodlands Valley. Keep to the path and eventually the path will fork - the choice of routes from here is entirely up to you, but whichever route you decide upon you will end up at Alport Bridge. Firstly, you can proceed along the path you are already on, passing close to the holding of Upper Ashop, then drop straight down from here to the footbridge spanning the River Ashop, then upwards to the Alport Bridge on the Snake road. Or secondly, you could go via the path that forks backwards to your right. This path swings round onto the stone Rowlee Bridge which also fords the Ashop. From there continue up the path onto the Snake road, turn left onto it and follow it up past the quaint 18th century Woodlands Chapel, standing in solitude on a small knoll. A little further up the road lays Alport Bridge the 6 mile (9kms.) point.

From the bridge continue up the Snake road for about 1 mile (1½kms.) where you will find to your left an access point into the valley below. Here you will find Blackden Barn, a very good landmark. Drop into the valley and cross over the footbridge. A good rest would not go amiss now for in front of you awaits a long undulating climb.

Rested and refreshed, proceed up the hill and over the ladder stile into the land of open access on Dean Hill. Follow the fence/wall on your right till you come upon Blackden Brook lying below you, go down to meet it at a small waterfall, the first of many and proceed up the brook. The walk now becomes increasingly steep but as with other walks this is offset by the scenic crags above and the numerous mini waterfalls that you pass. Care must be taken as you near the rocky upper region. You will leave the clough at the peaceful and tranquil Blackden Rind. Another well-deserved rest is advised here for you will have now covered 9 miles (14½kms.) with another 4 miles (6½kms.) left of your walk.

From Blackden Rind retrace your steps back to Edale as described at the end of Walk 2, via Hartshorn. If the weather is misty do not attempt the plateau route for Hartshorn, but make your way round Blackden Edge, on your left, which will eventually veer inwards after about six or seven minutes. Stop here and set your compass for due south and then proceed up onto the moor for the shortest stretch of the plateau, the Seven Minute Crossing. This quick route will bring you out at Dry Clough, to the right of Nether Tor. It is just a formality to just drop down this somewhat rocky clough into the Grindsbrook Valley and then Edale.

WALK 13 THE MIDDLE KINDER PLATEAU CIRCUIT

Length: 13 miles (21½kms.)
Start and Finish: Edale
Going: Bog trotting to firm, best attempted on a clear bright day
Gradient: Moderate at first then easy going
Time: 8 hours on average or 5 - 6 hours walking straight round.

It is advisable to leave this walk alone if there is any hint of mist, for a large section of it is on the plateau, an eerie place in mist, which can be quite dangerous even for experienced walkers. Once again, this is one of the walks that takes familiar ground from other routes, but you will notice that certain sections of the walk will be in reverse to the previous descriptions. This is a very scenic walk, recommended for all photography enthusiasts.

From the Edale starting point go to Grindsbrook Booth, over the log bridge at the start of the Pennine Way, then turning left over on the other side in the direction of Grindsbrook Clough. As you walk along you will notice over to your right a path rising up the hillside; this is the Nab which you duly ascend via this path and the steps provided for you. The climb is stiff and snake-like, but once you are up and standing on the Nab's shoulder taking in some excellent views, the climb will be forgotten.

From the shoulder turn about and follow the path in the direction of the craggy escarpment of the Ringing Roger. Near its base the path forks, the main route going on up the rocks of the Roger whilst the right-hand fork skirts around the base to the summit of the long Oller-brook Clough - this is the route you take. Upon reaching the Clough's summit turn left and follow the path that takes you along the longish escarpment of Ringing Roger. Note the fine views as you walk along here, as well as the different sorts of terrain you cross.

At the end of the Roger cross Golden Clough then go on to Nether Tor. On the western side of the tor is a small dry clough, aptly named Dry Clough, and using this as a marker turn to face inwards towards the plateau, then proceed due north over the Seven Minute Crossing. All being well you should come out over on the other side of the plateau on Blackden Edge.

Turn westwards following the edge around to the summit of Black-den Clough, Blackden Rind the 4 mile (6½kms.) point. Continue around the edge taking in the marvellous views of the valley below and the opposite moors whilst you pass the Seal Stones, Seal Edge and then onto the summit of the Fair Brook. Now follow the procedure as described in the middle section of Walk 4; the crossing of the plateau for the Downfall (west for a V-shape on the horizon, Kinder Down-fall).

The Downfall is reached after a 7½ mile (12kms.) walk, so a rest and some welcome nourishment would be about due!

With renewed vigour set off, retracing the course of the River Kinder back over the plateau, when you will pass through two large prominent rocks, just around the bend in the river. These rocks are the Kinder Gates. Continue along the river bed for about another ½ mile (1km.) until the river starts to peter out or, more correctly, where the River Kinder starts its formation. From this point take a bearing of 140° (S.S.E.) and start out over the plateau, your objective being the head of Crowden Brook. Depending on the time of the day, then you will either be heading into the sun or it will be to your right. If by chance you do get a bit worried as to your location do not panic, but carry on with your course or head straight for the sun, which will bring you out somewhere between Kinderlow End and the Woolpacks. On the other hand, if there is no sun, set your compass for due south and this will also bring you out somewhere along this section. These alternatives should only be used if you are really worried, for you can end up walking a lot farther across the plateau than on the original bearing.

Upon reached Crowden Brook head, follow the course down till you stand within the shadow of Crowden Tower. From now on it is plain sailing. Turn eastwards, following the path over Edale Moor to the head of the Grindsbrook Clough, then descend the scenic valley below to Grindsbrook Booth, and down the road back to Edale station.

WALK 14 THE EASTERN BOUNDARY CIRCUIT

Length: 10½ miles (18kms.)
Start and Finish: Edale
Going: Firm to more bog trotting
Gradient: Moderate or steep, depending on the middle route taken
Time: 5 - 6 hours on the shorter route, 6 - 7 hours on the longer route.

A pleasant walk that takes in a large slice of the Vale of Edale and a small section of the top of Kinder. Midway round the walk you have a choice of two routes, one being fairly strenuous the other very moderate. The most prominent feature of this walk is that it takes in a number of boundaries - National Trust boundaries, Open Access boundaries, ancient boundaries and village-cum-booth boundaries.

The starting point is Edale station/car park. Walk up to the Fieldhead Information Centre where you will find, just by it, a minor slip road. Divert onto this, crossing the stile at the bottom. Follow the footpath to the booth of Ollerbrook and its small companion Nether Ollerbrook, then proceed through the farming community, coming out once again onto farm grazing land. Follow the signposted path which meanders close to the smallholdings of Cotefield and Woodhouse Farm. The footpath finally ends at Nether Booth on the Hope road.

A pleasant walk along this road culminates at Edale End, the civil parish boundary of Edale and the start of Hope civil parish. To gain access to Edale End you will have to locate a railway bridge close by the Hope road; opposite this bridge on the left-hand side of the road you will notice a gate. Pass through the gate and down the banking to

Bagshaw Bridge. On the other side of the bridge lies Edale End, 3½ miles (6kms.) from Edale station.

Amble through this small community, which has also now become a boundary marker for the National Trust. Follow the path onto the ridge lying above you to your right; the old Roman road leading onto Hope Brink. The ridge having been attained turn once again to your left, heading for the old boundary marker of Hope Cross. Continue, passing through the gate and up to the signpost at the top of the small hill. A decision must now be made, for you have a choice of two routes, one being very straightforward the other more energetic.

Route One takes you up by Crookstone Barn and then on up Crookstone Hill by-passing an ancient cairn. In the distance, and rising up predominantly, lies the rocky Crookstone Knoll, your objective and the 6½ mile (10kms.) point.

Route Two goes by way of Jaggers' Clough. Take the route to Clough Farm that drops down the hillside, where you will come upon the brook flowing out from Jaggers' Clough at the boundary of open access (also the N.T. boundary line). The walk up Jaggers' Clough is both long and steep, but this is one of those cloughs that holds a certain charisma, rugged but pleasant. As you near the summit the brook cascades over the rocks creating mini waterfalls, whilst the scene behind you is one of the best of any clough. From the summit turn to your right, following the path round to Crookstone Knoll. Now that you have arrived at the knoll you will find it is an opportune time to rest and take in the magnificent view of the Woodlands Valley below, especially the N.W. end of the Ladybower Reservoir enshrouded by the tall conifer trees.

Your next objective is the Madwoman's Stones, boundary stones of the civil parishes of Hope and Edale. These stones are located S.W. of the knoll up the hill over thick moorland grasses and heather. You may be surprised, providing it is late spring or summer, how colourful the flora is around here with the large flat-topped rocks standing out in stark contrast. Looking S.W. again you will see on the horizon the O.S. pillar of Blackden Edge, boundary point of the N.T. and your next port of call. To gain access to the pillar a choice of two routes has to be made, either direct or indirect, the indirect being slightly longer but much safer. It follows the path along Blackden Edge, but the big disadvantage with this route is that the pillar goes out of sight and you have to judge where it is located then cross a short expanse of moor to reach it.

The more direct route is over the higher regions of Upper Moor, an inhospitable place full of thick peat and groughs as well as deep peat pools. You must take care in crossing and watch where you place your feet, staying well clear of the pools.

All the climbing is over with from this point. All that is left is the straightforward walk down to Edale. Set a course from the O.S. pillar due south. Directly over the next span of moor lies the picturesque escarpment of Ringing Roger, the open access boundary line. On attaining Ringing Roger turn westwards along its escarpment and continue to Golden Clough. Go directly down to its base where you will be confronted by the boundary of open access sign. Pass through the gate here, going on through the small wood then the pleasant little meadow overshadowed by flat-topped Nab. Cross the log bridge, official starting point of the long Pennine Way, coming out into Grindsbrook Booth at the Old Nag's Head Inn. A short walk down the road will bring you back to Edale station and the train or your car home.

WALK 15 THE FAR NORTHERN ARC

Length: 16½ miles (26kms.)
Start: Edale Finish: Hayfield
Going: A mixture of firm ground and some bog trotting. It is advisable not to attempt this walk in inclement weather
Gradient: Moderate
Time: 8 - 9 hours at a very steady pace.

The Northern Arc is quite an invigorating and strenuous walk which takes in some of the far northern points of the Kinder rim, including Lady Clough and the surrounding moorland, so you can expect quite a bit of bog trotting. Once again, sections of this walk will correspond with earlier sections from previous walks, most notably Walk 13, so you will have a fair idea what to expect. The walk starts at Edale and ends at Hayfield but it can be done in reverse; there is no advantage gradient wise.

Follow the opening of Walk 13 as far as the summit of The Nab, then turn to face Ringing Roger and advance to where the path forks right. Ignore this fork and keep going straight on and up the western flank of Ringing Roger which overlooks Golden Clough. Turn westwards on attaining the top of the Roger, crossing over Golden Clough where you now revert back to Walk 13, following the route from here across to Blackden Rind, the 3 mile (5kms.) point.

From the Rind make your way round to the shoulder of the Seal

Stones. As you come round onto the northern edge of the stones you should be able to locate a small straight clough lying just down the hill; this is Gate Side Clough, your route down into the Woodlands Valley. Through the clough there is a faint but discernible path that swings N.W. near the base of the clough and follows the River Ashop. A short and pleasant walk along the valley will bring you to the confluence of the Fair Brook with the River Ashop. Cross over the brook then the footbridge over the river, to gain access to the forest beyond. Follow the path through the forest till you come out on the Snake road close to the Snake Inn, where a brief respite is welcomed either inside or out. You will have now covered a moderate 6 miles (9kms.) with the most strenuous part lying in front of you.

From the Inn go up the Snake road for a few paces until you locate the access point for the Snake Path. Follow this back into the woodlands and round to the log bridge which fords the Lady Brook. You now leave the Snake Path behind, proceeding northwest back along the course of the Lady Brook into the heart of the thick Ladyclough Forest. Though the scenic escarpments and crags overlooking the wild moors are blotted out, the walk through the forest makes for contrast and is quite pleasant. The path ends at the most northern point of the forest, coming out onto the Snake road again.

A short walk up the road will bring you to an entry point into Lady Clough itself which lies to your left. Drop down to the clough's base where you will find yourself enclosed in a pleasant little valley, where there are several feeders for the brook cascading from beneath the Snake road. Follow the brook to the head of the valley where on your left you will notice a tight, narrow and steep clough down which tumbles another feeder for the Lady Brook; this is Thomason's Hollow. Prepare yourself now for some bog trotting! Scramble up Thomason's Hollow until you stand on its summit at Salvin Ridge. Now walk due south down the other side of the ridge, picking up another main feeder flowing down off the moor. This feeder will lead you into the Upper Gate Clough, which in turn ferries you back onto the Snake Path in the Ashop Valley. As you exit from the clough onto the Snake you will espy an old shooting cabin over to your right which is set in idyllic surroundings; a very good place to rest for a while after covering 10 miles (16kms.).

Refreshed and keen to be on your way, follow the Snake westwards through the Ashop Valley which is both scenic and boggy at certain points. The path swings round by Ashop Head, a bog riddled place, then continues on southwards down William Clough. From the bottom of the clough you will perceive a path going up the hill to your right, this is the continuation of the Snake Path and your route back into Hayfield. As you ascend the path you will notice the ever-widening amphitheatre opening out below you, whilst in front the path brings you to the white shooting cabin on Middle Moor. Continue along the main path, which is now somewhat flat, until it swings south again and drops into Hayfield via the Kinder road.

WALK 16 THE WESTERN CIRCUIT

Length: 15 miles (24kms.)
Start and Finish: Hayfield
Going: Firm with a lot of tangled undergrowth and some bog trotting
Gradient: Steep then moderate
Time: 9 hours is about normal.

The last three walks (16-18) are only recommended to the very hardy and experienced walker. This walk takes in the crest of Kinder and then the western moors, and whilst much of it will be on familiar ground the rest will be walked over terrain where there are bogs aplenty, encased within moorland grass and heather. This is one of those walks where it is not advisable to attempt it in very inclement weather.

Follow the opening of Walk 2 from Hayfield to the foot of William Clough, then follow the faint path up the western flanks of the Kinder massif. Your bearing up the path will be N.E. As you near the sumit after a long toil, the path peters out amongst a jumble of rocks. However, undeterred, make your way through them till you eventually crest them, and find yourself on the path close to the Upper Western Buttesss. You can take comfort in the thought that there will be no more climbing for quite a while.

Make your way S.E. by the flat-rock area of Sandy Heys, then onwards to the Kinder Downfall where you follow the river back to its first bend. Set your compass now to around 70° (a bearing of N.E.) and set off on this course over the plateau for your destination of Fairbrook Naze, roughly 20 -25 minutes over the peat hags. Your bearing of 70° takes in an allowance of a plus and minus to come out on any point of the long naze. Once Fairbrook Naze has been reached you will enjoy a good long rest after covering 6 miles (9kms.) of climbing and bog trotting!

Once refreshed, turn westwards to walk along The Edge taking in the panoramic view of the valley below and the opposite moors. Your journey along The Edge culminates at the N.W. buttress of Kinder where it overlooks Mill Hill on the other side of the small valley. Drop down off Kinder to cross the boggy valley, then proceed up Mill Hill till you stand on the summit; a short rest is advised here whilst you take stock of the situation that now confronts you. Study your map, for the next part of the walk lies over the tangled moorland of Leygatehead Moor which takes up a large slice of the six miles left.

Your route lies over the northern fringes of the moor and you must at all times keep to the main path that bears west over the moor. Your objective is Burnt Hill where - providing it is summer - you will find to your amazement all the different coloured flora that flourishes around the summit of the hill; a welcome change from the dark and dismal Leygatehead.

Blind man's buff is the name of the game for the next section, because there is no path of any description to follow to your next scenic point, Hollingworth Waterfall. Bear S.S.E. down the hill, which is very hard and trying, until you pick up a feeder brook flowing directly south. Keep to this brook which will eventually bring you to the splendid waterfall. With luck you may even notice the waterfall as you come down off Burnt Hill before you meet up with the feeder. If the day is sunny and warm the waterfall looks tantalizingly inviting - however, you must press on. Your route now follows the course of the brook down to the footbridge at Carr Meadow about 1 mile (1½kms.) downstream. Another rest would not go amiss at Carr Meadow, a very idyllic place, before you set off on the last leg.

Cross the footbridge to stand on its southern end then stride out up the hill in front of you, keeping to the path. As you reach the top of the hill you will notice to your left The Knot which rises above you. (If you do not feel tired and time permits then I recommend you climb to its cairn-topped summit, where you will perceive an excellent panoramic view of a complete 360° sweep. Away to the S.E. you will be able to see the white shooting cabin of Middle Moor; make your way down and over to this point.) Those of you who do not fancy the climb up to The Knot will continue round the base onto Middle Moor, keeping to the path, where it leads you up to a long footbridge which spans a deep bog. Once across you will be at the shooting cabin. Your way back to Hayfield now lies over the moor via the Snake Path which drops down onto Kinder road, and a very short walk to the bus and home.

WALK 17 THE BIG TOP

Length: 25 miles (40kms.)
Start and Finish: Hayfield (but see below)
Going: Basically firm
Gradient: Very Moderate
Time: 10 - 12 hours.

For the last two walks you will take on Kinder in two different scopes, the upper edges and the skirting of the base. This walk takes in all the edges around the top of the Kinder massif. It is one of the three walks recommended only to the competent walker. This walk and the next can start from any accessible point, for they must finish where you started to complete the circles; ideally suited for the motorist provided he or she studies the access points and route carefully. If you use public transport check the times of your bus or train home, then you will know at what pace and time to set yourself. All the terrain and land you will be walking over will already have been covered in the various walks previous to this one. For a very good reason which will be revealed later on, I will describe the route starting at Hayfield (or if you are travelling by car, Bowden Bridge Quarry, Hayfield).

From the Information Centre make your way over to Kinder road, go along to Bowden Bridge Quarry, turn right and follow the road round to Coldwell Clough, continuing up to Stonyford then up to Edale Cross. At the Cross bear north following the dry-stone wall up the hill until you reach the foot of the Swine's Back, then wind your way up onto the plateau of the Swine's Back proceeding then to follow the edge round eastwards. Drop down to the path below which continues on a bearing N.E. past the Noe Stool then into the Woolpacks. Pressing on through these magnificent rocks you pass by Crowden Tower, cross over Crowden Brook then continue along the path making for the head of Grindsbrook Clough. Once reached, swing round northwards locating a fording place between the Grindsbrook Towers. On the other side turn to come around the eastern tower's shoulder, following the path over the tors of Far Upper, Upper and Nether. Cross over Golden Clough to gain access to the excellent escarpment of the Ringing Roger which in due course will bring you onto the escarpment above Rowland Cote Moor and consequently the Druids' Stone. Here you will find no better place along this edge to have a well-earned rest whilst taking in the rugged beauty of the land around you, and you can reflect upon the 9 miles (14½kms.) already covered.

Leaving Druids' Stone behind, keep to the path that swings around the higher regions of the Upper Moor, across Jaggers' Clough summit

The perimeter path on Kinder, looking towards Blackden Edge.

then N.E. for Crookstone Knoll. It is from here that you start the longer journey back to Hayfield. Keep to the path that meanders along Blackden Edge overlooking the picturesque Woodlands Valley until you reach Blackden Rind. The path now continues on around the shoulder of the Seal Stones, then to Seal Edge, down and across the summit of the Fair Brook, then north to the nose of Fairbrook Naze where another rest will once again be welcomed at the 15 mile (24kms.) point.

The Edge now awaits your pleasure. Swinging round at the end to crest the Mill Hill Rocks, then bear S.E. over the Upper Western Buttress, Sandy Heys and Kinder Downfall.

The reason why I chose this particular way round now becomes clear. Providing it is a sunny evening, the Downfall is bathed in the rays of the setting sun, taking on a golden-brown hue as the light shines directly onto the rockface and the waterfall glistens as it cascades into the valley below. As the green pasture land takes on a richer texture, what better setting could you have to renew your sapping strength?

From the Downfall take the path south over the Red Brook summit where once again visions of Kinder Downfall are perceived in the evening sun. Continue on until you reach the O.S. pillar of Kinder Low where you now make your way down to the right-hand side of the Edale Rocks. Pass them by going down to the dry-stone wall, turn in the direction of the Swine's Back then follow the Pennine Way route down to the signpost below.

Carry on up the opposite hill in the direction of Brown Knoll whereupon attaining the hill's summit cross over the fencing at one of the stiles, then proceed on your way keeping the fence to your left. Eventually you will come between the hills of Mount Famine and South Head, but meanwhile over to your right you will be able to see Kinder in the setting of the sun; a sight highly recommended.

From South Head swing round on the path until you come round the back of Mount Famine, then proceed through a gate onto Highgate where you continue (with a last glimpse of Kinder over to your right) into Hayfield - absolutely shattered!

WALK 18 THE KINDER CLASSIC (KINDER ROUND)

Length: 25 miles (40kms.)
Start and Finish: Edale (but see below)
Going: Firm but a couple of bogs
Gradient: Negligible
Time: 10 - 12 hours.

And last but not least we come to the Kinder Round, and what a walk it is! Not for the faint hearted, for surprisingly it is a lot tougher than The Big Top itself. The walk is commonly known as the Kinder Round but many walkers regard this as the classic walk of Kinder, if not the classic walk of the High Peak. In contrast to the previous walk this one skirts the entire base of Kinder and is generally begun in the west and followed anti-clockwise on the map. However, this does not allow you the freedom to drop out, except at Edale when you will only have covered about a quarter of the walk. If you start in the east, however, then by the time you have reached the Hayfield area you will have covered three-quarters of the walk and escape is feasible if you are tired or it is getting late. Hayfield and Edale are the only places you can go for public transport. Of course, if you are a motorist you will have little choice but to complete the walk.

Nearly all the route to be attempted has already been described in detail on previous walks.

The starting point of this strenuous walk is Edale station/car park. Follow the opening of Walk 14, Fieldhead Information Centre, Ollerbrook Booth then onto Nether Booth. Proceed up the road through the booth until you reach the old Ashopton - Derwent Woodlands village signpost, described in more detail in Walk 12. Keeping to Walk 12, follow the route as described from this point - Clough Farm, around Nether Moor, Jaggers' Clough then up the opposite banking to the signpost near Crookstone Barn. Still keeping with Walk 12, carry on to Blackley Clough, Blackley Hey, Upper Ashop Farm then down to the footbridge over the River Ashop, proceeding then up the opposite bank to the Snake road and the Alport Bridge.

You now leave Kinder behind you because the next section lies across Cowms Moor, on the fringes of the Bleaklow massif. The reason for this is that there is no recognised complete path along these lower regions between Alport Bridge and the Snake Inn, a distance of about 2 miles (3kms.). Also the main bulk of this area around the River Ashop belongs to the Derwent and Trent Waterboard and is private. This gives you two options, either to walk up the Snake road to the Inn, with the disadvantage of having to frequently dodge passing cars, or walk over the Doctor's Gate Track; an extension of the Hope Brink Roman road which meanders over the quiet and often picturesque Cowm Moor. This route is more leg sapping than going the Snake road way, so pick you own route!

From Alport Bridge turn into Alport Dale where you will immediately find to your left a path going up the hillside. Follow this path until you meet a path again coming up from your left; bear onto this which takes you down behind Hayridge Farm. From the farm until you reach Oyster Clough the path is somewhat straight, running parallel to the Snake road but overlooked by the Cowms Rocks. A number of stiles have to be crossed. Nearing Oyster Clough the path swings upwards to your right, then drops down into the clough itself. Scale the opposite bank, rejoining the path at the top which you duly follow through the fringes of the forest till you reach the rocky outcrop of Dinas Sitch Tor. A path will be located to your left which drops sharply through the forest, coming out onto the Snake road a little way up from the Snake Inn. Across the road lies the access point for the Snake Path, your next stage - but first a little respite and refreshment, for the inn is quite handy for those who want to reach other parts that no one else can reach!

Set off on the long meandering Snake Path, through the forest, over the Saukin Ridge then on and out into the Ashop Valley. Keep to the path all the way through the valley then on round the peat-sodden bog land of Ashop Head. Once past here you press on between the N.W. buttress of Kinder and Mill Hill and down through William Clough, round The Nab, and on to White Brow with the pleasant Kinder Reservoir lying to your left. Exit at the reservoir gates and then proceed over the footbridge, to go up the opposite hill and come out above Farlands. (Those of you who have had enough can now veer off to Hayfield. Do not feel disgraced or downhearted, for many a person has set off on this walk and not completed it the first time.)

Revert now to the beginning of Walk 8 for a more detailed description of the next section which takes you to the access point of open country at Broad Clough. Go through the gate then turn to your right, continuing on your way between the two dry-stone walls. Go round the base of Kinderlow end via another gate, and round the shoulder of Kinderlow until you reach Stonyford. Cross the brook, making your way up the hill to Edale Cross where you will be glad to know that you have just negotiated your last climb.

Your way from the cross lies downwards. It drops onto Jacob's Ladder then down again over the old packhorse bridge on Yongate, where you stand at the beginning of Lee Estate and the Vale of Edale. A straightforward walk now confronts you as the path leads into Upper Booth. Those who were disappointed at Edale Cross to learn that there was to be no more climbing can veer off here and proceed through the booth and farmyard then upwards onto the flanks of Broadlee Bank Tor, coming out at Grindsbrook Booth. Those who prefer the more sedate route will carry on, by-passing the booth, following the track through to Barber Booth and the Hope - Edale road, where a short walk will bring you back to Edale station and a nice restful journey home.

REGIONAL INFORMATION

TOURIST INFORMATION CENTRES:

Main office: Peak National Park, Baslow Road, Bakewell, Derbyshire. DE4 1AE. Tel: (0622981) 4321.
Edale: Fieldhead. Tel: Hope Valley (0433) 70207.
Castleton: Castle Street. Tel: Hope Valley (0433) 20679.
Glossop: Rail bus terminus. Tel: Glossop 5920.
Sheffield: Central Library. Tel: Sheffield 734760.
Hayfield: Sett Valley. Tel: 0663 46222.

For courses on conservation of the Peak etc. and activity holiday centre contact:

The Principal, Peak National Park Study Centre, Lose Hill Hall, Castleton, Derbyshire. S30 2WB. Tel:Hope Valley (0433) 20373 office (0433) 20568 visitors.

CAVING:

National Caving Association, Hon. Sec. c/o Department of Geography, The University, P.O. Box 363, Birmingham. B15 3TT.
Derbyshire Caving Association, East Midlands Area Office, 26 Musters Road, West Bridgeford, Nottingham.

NATIONAL TRUST ESTATE OFFICE:

Edale End, Edale Road, Hope via Sheffield. Tel: Hope Valley (0433) 70368.

RAMBLERS' ASSOCIATION:

Edale area contact The Ramblers' Inn, Edale. Tel: Hope Valley (0433) 70268.

PENNINE WAY BUREAU: Tel: (0274) 598263.

EDALE RANGER SERVICE: Fieldhead, Edale. Tel: Hope Valley (0433) 70207.

MOUNTAIN RESCUE: Contact the nearest Police Station or Fieldhead.

WEATHERLINE:

Peak District and South Yorkshire: Tel: (0742) 8091.
Edale: Tel: (0433) 70207.

EDALE ADVENTURE HOLIDAYS: Contact The Warren, Edale. S30 2ZY. Tel: (0433) 70256.

LADYBOOTH PONY TREKKING CENTRE: (Nether Booth) Tel: (0433) 70205.

PEAK CYCLE HIRE:
Hayfield: Information Centre. Tel: (0663) 46222.
Derwent: Fairholmes picnic site. Tel: (0433) 51261.

PEVERIL CASTLE, CASTLETON: Tel: (0433) 20613.

RAMBLERS' INN, EDALE: Tel: (0433) 70268.

NAG'S HEAD INN, EDALE: Tel: (0433) 70212.

CAVES AND MINES OF CASTLETON:
Blue John: Tel: (0433) 20638/20642.
Speedwell: Tel: (0433) 20512.
Peak Cavern: Tel: (0433) 20285.
Treak Cliff: Tel: (0433) 20571.

HOSTELS:
Youth Hostel Association Regional Office, 38 Bank Road, Matlock, Derbyshire. Tel: (0629) 4666.

High Peak Hostels, in all cases contact The Warden.
Castleton: Castleton Hall, Castleton, Sheffield. Tel: (0433) 20636
Crowden: Peak National Park Hostel, Crowden, Hadfield, Hyde, Cheshire. Tel: Glossop (04574) 2135.
Edale: Rowland Cote, Nether Booth, Edale. Tel: (0433) 70302.
Ashopton: Hagg Farm, Ashopton, Bamford, Sheffield. S30 2BJ. Tel: (0433) 51594.
Hathersage: Castleton Road, Hathersage, Sheffield.
Langsett: Y.H.A. Langsett, Stocksbridge, Sheffield.

CARAVAN AND CAMPSITES:
Hagg Farm Hostel. Tel: (0433) 51594.
Hathersage, North Lees Hall. Tel: (0433) 50838.
Hayfield: Tel: New Mills 45394.
Castleton, Losehill Hall. Tel: (0433) 20636.
Crowden: Tel: (2127) 66057.
Edale, Fieldhead: (tents only please) Tel: (0433) 70372.
Edale, Newbold Farm: Tel: (0433) 70372.

Edale, Whitmore Lea Farm: Tel: (0433) 70238.
Edale, Waterside Farm: Tel: (0433) 70215.
Edale, Upper Booth Farm: Tel: (0433) 70250.
Edale, Ollerbrook Farm: Tel: (0433) 70235.

CAMPING BARNS:
Castleton, Losehill Barn: Grid Ref.153838. Tel: (0433) 20373.
Ladybower, Alport Castles Barn: Grid Ref.135910. Tel: (0433) 50934.

BED AND BREAKFAST, EDALE:
Cotefield Farm: Tel: (0433) 70273.
Carr House: Tel: (0433) 20018.
The Warren: Tel: (0433) 70256.
The Vicarage: Tel: (0433) 70254.
Newlands: Tel: (0433) 70288.
Graylings: Tel: (0433) 70226.

Part of the main bulk of the Liberator wreckage, Mill Hill

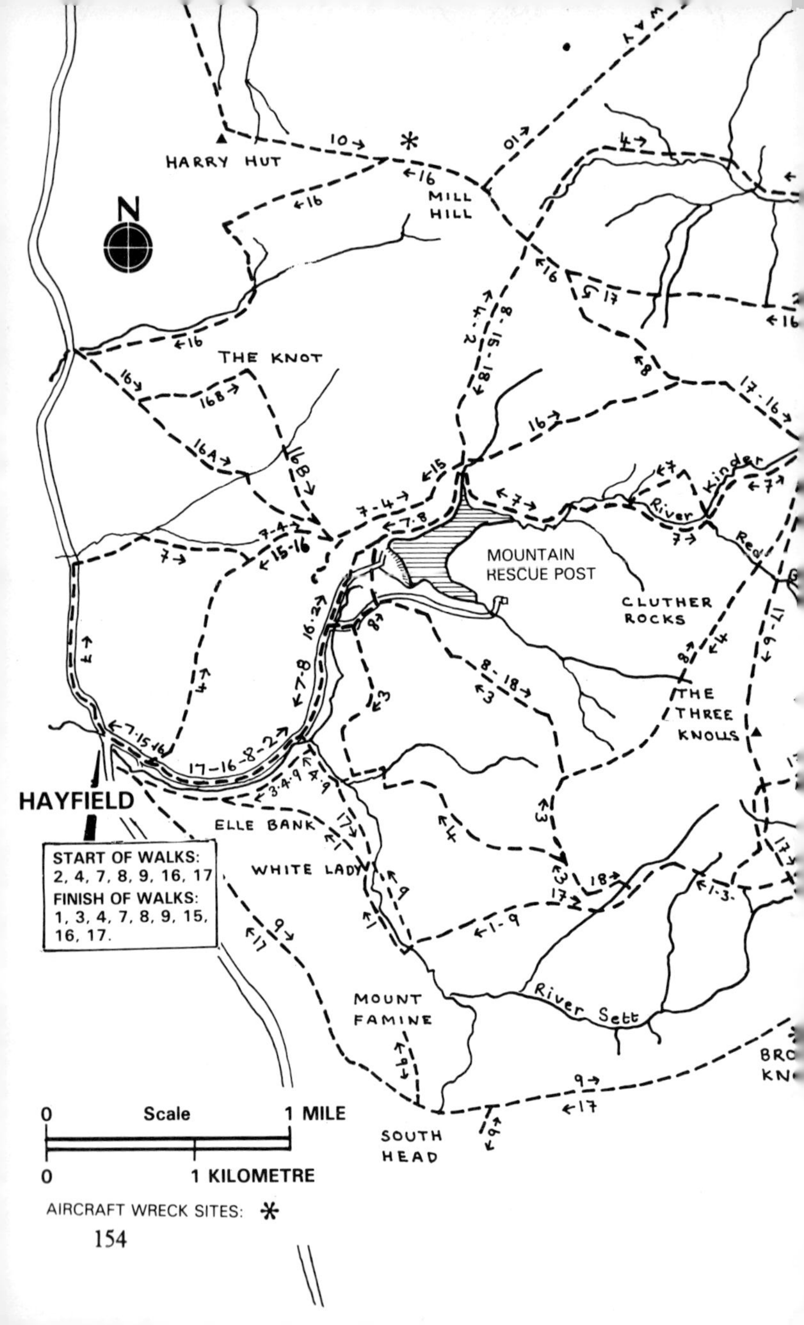
N
HARRY HUT
MILL HILL
THE KNOT
MOUNTAIN RESCUE POST
CLUTHER ROCKS
River Kinder
THE THREE KNOLLS
HAYFIELD
ELLE BANK
WHITE LADY
START OF WALKS:
2, 4, 7, 8, 9, 16, 17
FINISH OF WALKS:
1, 3, 4, 7, 8, 9, 15, 16, 17.
River Sett
MOUNT FAMINE
SOUTH HEAD
0 Scale 1 MILE
0 1 KILOMETRE
AIRCRAFT WRECK SITES: *

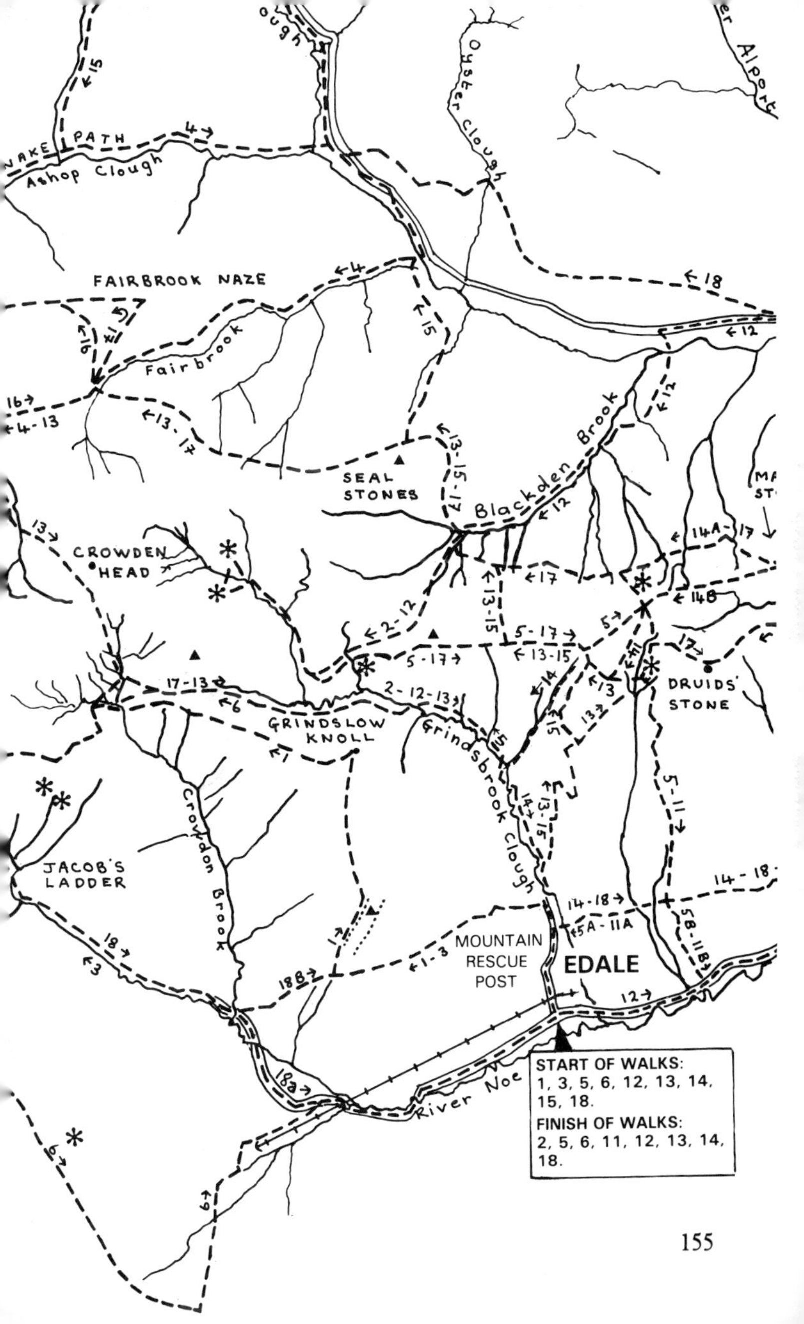
NAKE PATH
Ashop Clough
Oyster Clough
Alport
FAIRBROOK NAZE
Fairbrook
SEAL
STONES
Blackden Brook
CROWDEN
HEAD
GRINDSLOW
KNOLL
Grindsbrook Clough
DRUIDS'
STONE
JACOB'S
LADDER
Crowdon Brook
MOUNTAIN
RESCUE
POST
EDALE
River Noe
START OF WALKS:
1, 3, 5, 6, 12, 13, 14, 15, 18.
FINISH OF WALKS:
2, 5, 6, 11, 12, 13, 14, 18.

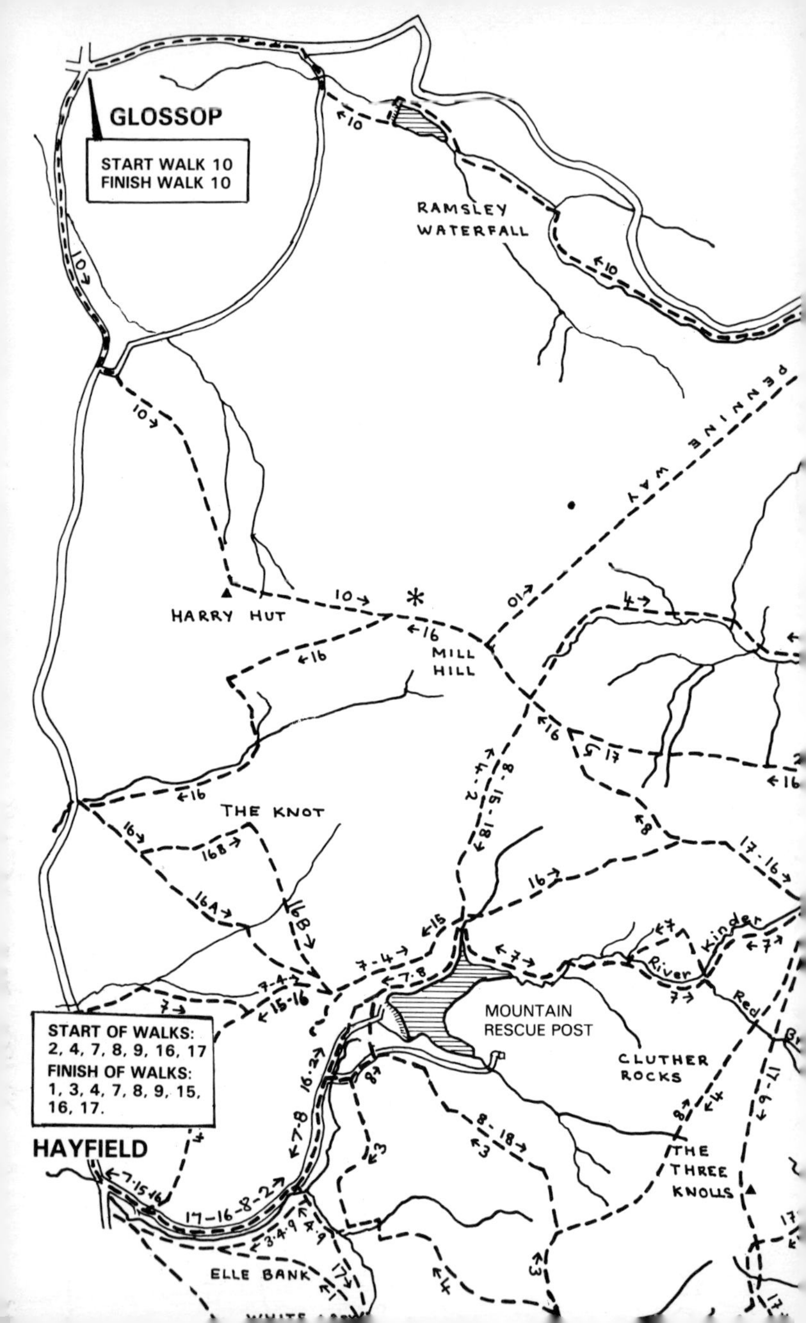
GLOSSOP
START WALK 10
FINISH WALK 10
RAMSLEY
WATERFALL
PENNINE WAY
HARRY HUT
MILL
HILL
THE KNOT
MOUNTAIN
RESCUE POST
CLUTHER
ROCKS
River Kinder
Red Brook
START OF WALKS:
2, 4, 7, 8, 9, 16, 17
FINISH OF WALKS:
1, 3, 4, 7, 8, 9, 15,
16, 17.
HAYFIELD
THE
THREE
KNOLLS
ELLE BANK

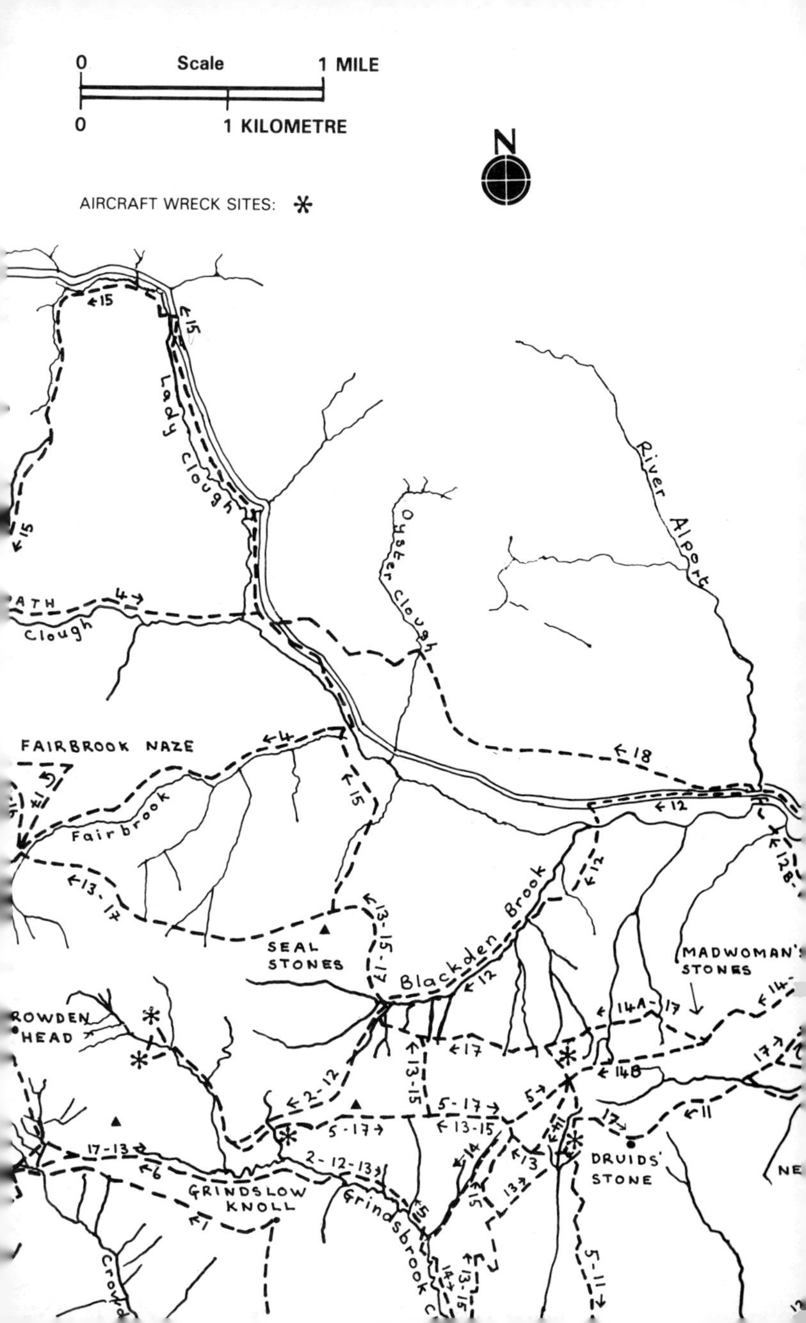

0
Scale
1 MILE
0
1 KILOMETRE
N
AIRCRAFT WRECK SITES: *
Lady Clough
River Alport
Oyster Clough
PATH
Clough
FAIRBROOK NAZE
Fairbrook
SEAL STONES
Blackden Brook
MADWOMAN'S STONES
ROWDEN HEAD
GRINDSLOW KNOLL
Grindsbrook
DRUIDS' STONE
Crowd

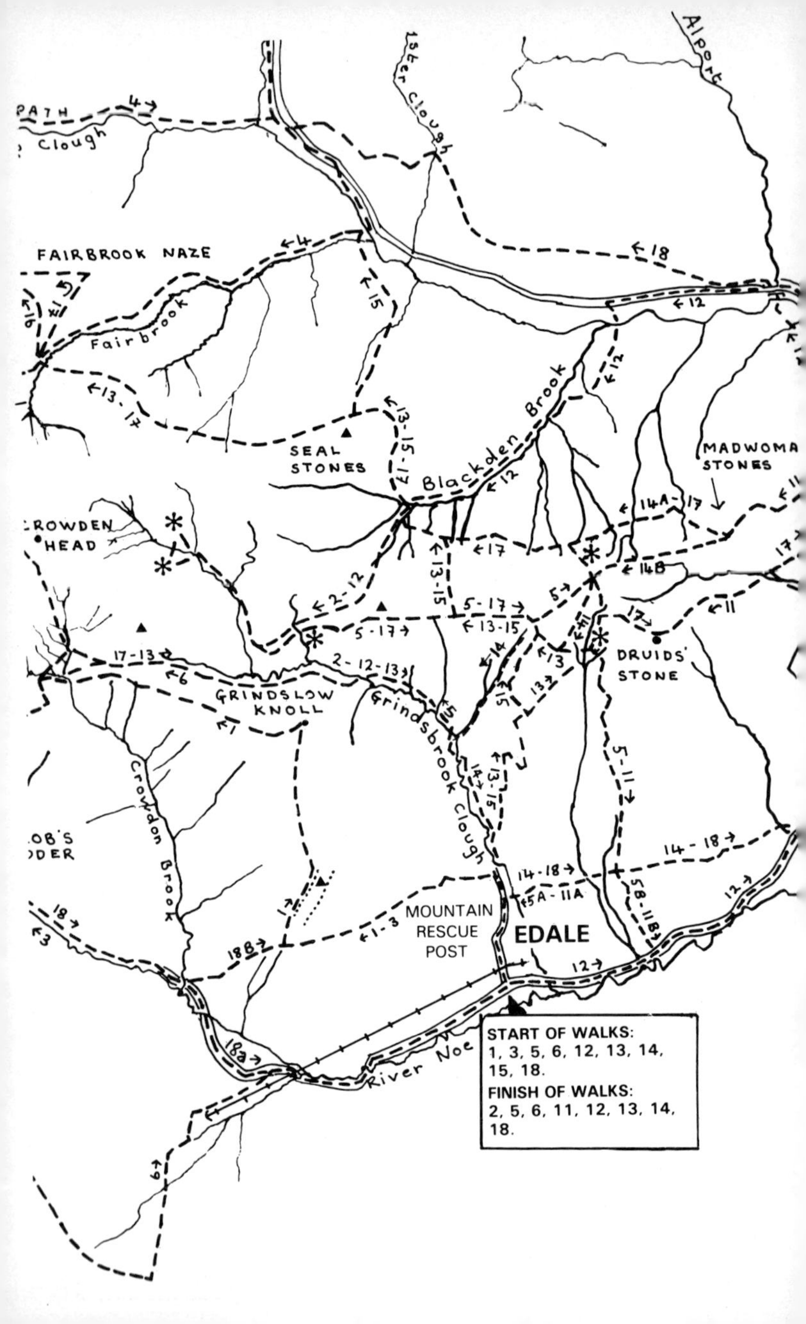

FAIRBROOK NAZE
Fairbrook
SEAL STONES
Blackden Brook
MADWOMA
STONES
CROWDEN HEAD
DRUIDS' STONE
GRINDSLOW KNOLL
Grindsbrook Clough
Crowdon Brook
MOUNTAIN RESCUE POST
EDALE
River Noe
START OF WALKS:
1, 3, 5, 6, 12, 13, 14, 15, 18.
FINISH OF WALKS:
2, 5, 6, 11, 12, 13, 14, 18.

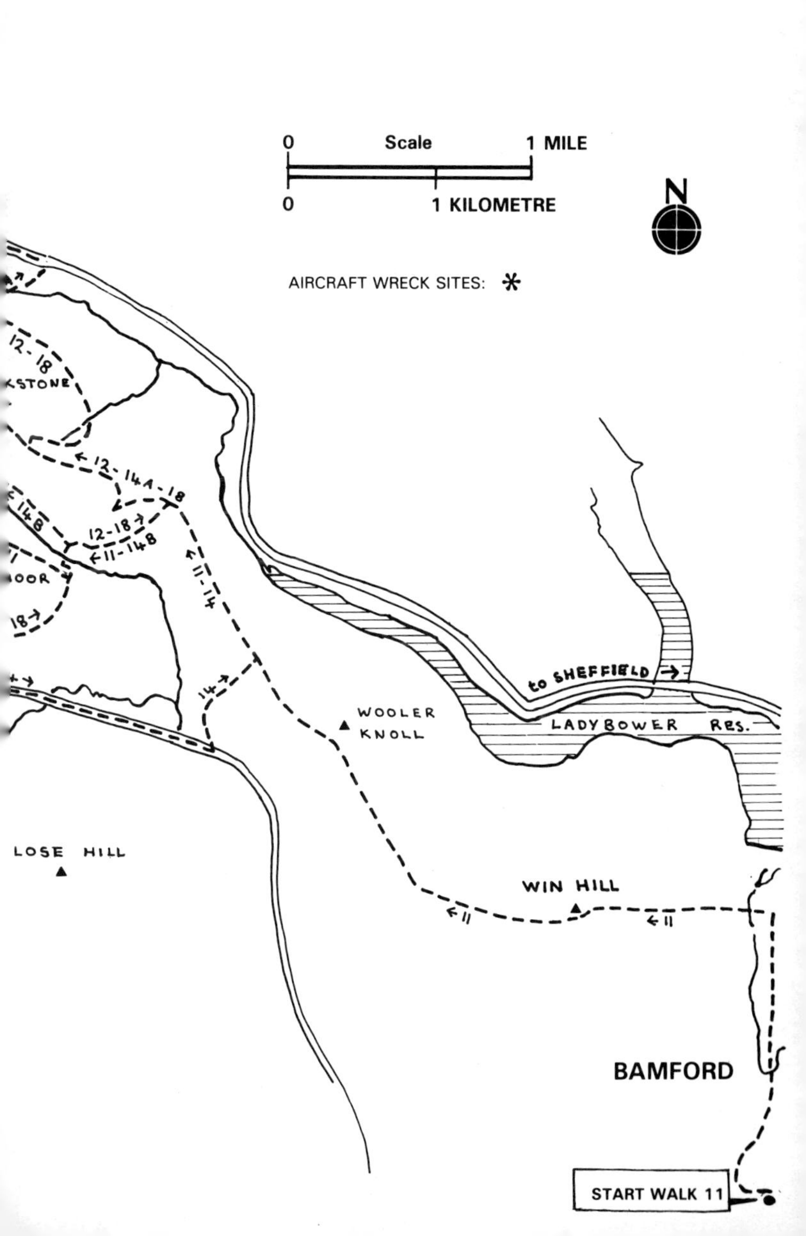
0
Scale
1 MILE
0
1 KILOMETRE
N
AIRCRAFT WRECK SITES: *
12-18
KSTONE
12-14A-18
14B
12-18
11-14B
11-14
OOR
18
14
WOOLER
KNOLL
to SHEFFIELD
LADYBOWER RES.
LOSE HILL
WIN HILL
11
11
BAMFORD
START WALK 11

IF YOU LIKE ADVENTUROUS ACTIVITIES ON MOUNTAINS OR HILLS YOU WILL ENJOY READING:

CLIMBER

MOUNTAINEERING/HILLWALKING/TREKKING SCRAMBLING/ROCK CLIMBING/ IN BRITAIN AND ABROAD

AVAILABLE FROM NEWSAGENTS, OUTDOOR EQUIPMENT SHOPS, OR BY SUBSRIPTION (6-12 MONTHS) FROM HOLMES MCDOUGALL LTD., RAVENSEFT HOUSE, 302-304 ST. VINCENT'S STREET, GLASGOW G2 5RG

THE WALKERS' MAGAZINE

the great OUTDOORS

COMPULSIVE MONTHLY READING FOR ANYONE INTERESTED IN WALKING

Available from your newsagent, outdoor equipment shop or on subscription from:
Holmes McDougall Ltd., Ravenseft House, 302/304 St. Vincent Street, Glasgow G2/5NL

Printed by Carnmor Print & Design,
95/97, London Road, Preston, Lancashire.